A Preface to Literary Analysis

SHELDON P. ZITNER • JAMES D. KISSANE • MYRON M. LIBERMAN

GRINNELL COLLEGE

SCOTT, FORESMAN AND COMPANY

CONTENTS

L. C. Catalog No. 64-25733
Copyright © 1964 by Scott, Foresman and Company, Glenview, Illinois 60025.
All rights reserved.
Printed in the United States of America.
Regional offices of Scott, Foresman and Company are located in
Atlanta, Dallas, Glenview, Palo Alto, and Oakland, N.J.

We have written this book for readers who want to refine their understanding of literature. It is neither "elementary" nor "advanced," for no one is wholly ignorant of literature, and in literary study a hard tug at any thread starts to unravel the center. But we have tried to deal with the most persistent questions of literary analysis and interpretation, and to deal with them in a way that will not weary scholars with the obvious or defeat students with the esoteric. Yet we make no apology for bringing up matters an intelligent student will not have thought of or a good teacher may find unnecessary. Mastering a discipline is in part learning where even the simplest questions may —surprisingly—lead.

Primarily, we have tried to present some of the distinctions and skills necessary in literary analysis. In the first chapter we treat the uses of literature itself, and in the three following chapters its major kinds—lyric, narrative, and drama—specifically, their management of language, point of view, character, and events. Though character and plot are considered under drama, and language and point of view under lyric or narrative, each of these topics is seen as relevant to all three genres. The remaining chapters of the book attempt an introduction to "close reading," applications of the previous discussions to passages from three quite different works and, finally, expositions of the premises of literary criticism.

We have tried to present all these matters clearly and systematically, allowing no term without definition, no generalization without example; and arranging all materials not only in logical categories but, as far as possible, in order of increasing difficulty. Moreover, we have tried to present them simply and in a style that does not belie the delights of literature itself.

We have also tried to make accessible here some of the insights and attitudes of recent literary criticism. Footnotes and allusions only imperfectly record our debts. We hasten to say, however, that this book is neither an anthology of recent opinion nor a least common denominator of classroom practice. In the course of reconciling positions or demonstrating insights, we were forced to rethink (and abandon) many commonplaces, and to open questions that—so far as we know—have been only indifferently considered. Our colleagues will, we fear, ruefully grant us more than our proper share of "originality." But the result of our conserving and our inventing is, we hope, a book that will free both instructor and student for extended and detailed consideration of literature itself.

Although this book is the result of a collaborative effort throughout, Chapter II is the work of Mr. Kissane and Chapter III the work of Mr. Liberman. Chapter VI is their joint effort. Mr. Zitner is responsible for Chapters I, IV, V, and VII. All of us have profited greatly from the tact and intelligence of our editor, Miss Judith Gregg, and from the help of the staffs of the Grinnell College and Newberry Libraries. Our thanks go also to three dauntless typists, Lynda Brayman, Ellen Crandall, and Jacqueline Swafford.

Chapter One   I   *Literature and the Humanities*

,too, dislike it: there are things that
are important beyond all this fiddle.

This line begins Marianne Moore's poem on poetry, which goes
on to say of literature that

> Reading it, however, with a perfect con-
> tempt for it, one discovers in
> it after all, a place for the genuine,

for things that are

> important not because a
> high-sounding interpretation can be put
> upon them but because they are
> useful.[1]

Our animal grasp of what is physically necessary and our common sense about what pays often persuade us how absurd it
is to stare half the night at slips of wood pulp, smiling or griev-
ing over them as though they were alive. To alter Hamlet's
question, What are we to Hecuba and what's Hecuba or even
Hamlet himself to us that we should weep for them? This is the
persistent question about literary study. How can one justify it
as human behavior? The question logically precedes questions
about literary study as a discipline. Since the study of literature

1   "Poetry," *Collected Poems* (New York: Macmillan, 1951), pp. 40–41.

is not unique as a kind of human behavior, but shares absurdities and uses with all the humanities, the question precedes particular problems in disciplines like philosophy and the fine arts as well. In this discussion we will try to reason out a way from the apparent absurdities of the humanities, and of literary study in particular, to their uses.

THE VAGUENESS AND CONTROVERSY OF THE HUMANITIES

Some of the fiddle we dislike about the humanities is their seeming vagueness and continual controversy. Philosophers today appear no closer to agreement on definitions of terms than were Socrates and his judges. Milton's phrase "two-handed engine" was at last count differently explained in essays from forty-two scholarly hands. And often enough one critic's masterpiece is another's trash. By contrast, the sciences appear to have a grandmotherly solidity. From China to Peru, everybody's e predictably equals mc^2, and disagreements in the sciences move with apparent calm through experiment to certainty.

Yet these are appearances only, and deeper acquaintance reveals more light in the humanities, more heat in the sciences, than do first impressions. There are several reasons why such first impressions are distorted: We are taught the elements of the sciences later than the elements of the humanities; hence we reach the controversial in literature and the arts when we are still receiving, quite passively, primary scientific information we are in no position to dispute. Moreover, practical considerations restrain us from arguing against the conventionally established speed of light, while any man with the price of a Penguin can own much of the "apparatus" he needs to dispute a criticism of *Hamlet*.

But a more important reason is that, while science does not ultimately treat certainties, the humanities actually and immediately do treat the problematical. They treat of Man; they attempt to know the seeker after knowledge through the works by which he seeks it, for the humanities treat of philosophy and the arts—of the great works of men. Yet it is impossible to be at one and the same time the observer and the observed without one role interfering with the other. Such is the problem raised by humanistic study, and it is not very useful to urge "objectivity" as a solution. Man is no object. And scientists—as well as humanists—have abandoned the nineteenth-century illusion that it is possible to make observations wholly apart from the subjectivity of the observer or the observed. Both the sciences and the humanities are involved in the problematic and the relative: not merely because they concern topics which are new, but because they approach the ultimate mysteries of life, where the data for "solutions" encroach upon the "problems" to be solved. If for this reason alone, we must expect differing opinions in humanistic studies.

Such differences are not merely inevitable; they are desirable. They no more imply ignorance than agreement implies knowledge. There was a time when people agreed that the sun flew round the earth (as obviously it does) and that toad's blood applied at midnight was the wonder drug for warts. Differences, we must hope, are often only signs of a perseverance in the revision of knowledge.

But controversy and revision are not the peculiar afflictions of the humanities. Textbooks in the sciences, though copyright yesterday, are already in question or out of date. In a memorable comment on the unending work of understanding literature, the poet John Dryden said: "The last verse is not yet sufficiently explicated." Nor is the last atomic particle, or the last election. This is not to say that we are doomed to a perpetual bondage of ignorance. Rather we should believe that "the spirit of *liberty* is the spirit that is not quite sure."

In any case, the uses of unanimity are largely mechanical. Unanimity may ratify a policy, but it cannot invent one. No majority, however large, ever wrote a sonata or added a single element to the periodic table. But difference has uses that are truly human. From it arise the great intellectual virtues: the self-knowledge and tolerance that come from plumbing the variety of others; the alertness that comes from prolonged exchange on common topics. Through what Bertrand Russell calls "hilarious Olympian controversy" we can hope to make ourselves not only more knowledgeable but more human. So we ought to give disagreement a good welcome.

But we ought not to consider the desirability of disagreement an invitation to the fashionable sluggishness of Pope's question: Who shall decide when doctors disagree? Very often teachers of the humanities expect different answers only because they have asked different questions. They agree substantially on what a work contains, though they may differ on its value or implications. Finally, they can agree upon the relative solidity of one criticism of a work, though they may ultimately prefer another.

Having said this much, we must appear to reverse ourselves and say that if difference is necessary to the growth of the intellectual virtues and to the process by which knowledge is mastered and revised, it is some large measure of agreement that is a goal of that process. General agreement to the notion that the sun goes round the earth was (in retrospect) certainly in error, but general agreement (now) is the basis of the view that the earth goes round the sun. We cannot "see" this revolution directly for ourselves; we "agree" that it is so. We cannot read all the books or perform all the experiments. From this arises the paradox of the process of knowing: learning requires both the disagreement from which the intellectual virtues grow and the agreement by which knowledge is validated and transmitted.

We all suffer this paradox of learning. Immediate goals of knowledge, when we reach them, are only momentarily satisfying. In agreement, we yawn. Only the next dispute, the next confession that we are not quite sure, really interests us. So we must go to the disputed frontiers of knowledge as soon as possible and waste no time in "futile" agreement. In this journey, course-work serves as guide.

DEFINING THE HUMANITIES

Courses in humanistic subjects are designed to promote the mastery and revision of that particular realm of study and the acquisition of the intellectual virtues that may arise from such an effort. But these intellectual virtues may arise from the disinterested pursuit of almost any subject. So we must discover the particular uses of the humanities. And to discover these uses we must consider what the humanities are.

Because of their long history, the humanities have been often defined through a catalog of their original component fields. Among these fields are the study of literature and of the fine arts, the study of philosophy and, when their objects are considered as works of the imagination rather than as applications of technique or accumulations of fact, such fields as architecture and history. But individual fields of knowledge change as knowledge as a whole grows and alters. New disciplines emerge from old ones; so the social sciences emerged like Chinese wooden dolls out of the belly of History. Disciplines, both old and new, continually change; so mathematics has altered the shape of philosophy. The confusion and doubt of one age become the curriculum of another. D. C. Allen puts it wittily when he tells us that in the eighteenth century "the humanist read Homer and Horace, looked through his telescope, collected birds' eggs . . . was kind to his servants, and wrote bad verse."[2] The verse may not have improved, but nowadays the birds at least are safe from humanists. In the course of such losses and gains, the humanities have been transformed. They can no longer be defined very usefully in terms of their origins or of the fields in which humanists are now at work. Perhaps no other way of defining them is much better. Yet it is useful to characterize the particular operations and habits of mind proper to the humanities.

The humanities treat the qualities of the great works of men and how these qualities are organized or related to one another.[3] They are to be distinguished from the sciences, which treat the qualities and organization of nature, and from the social studies, which treat the qualities and organization of human associations and institutions. These are the three great realms of study. None is reducible to any of the others. One cannot hope to understand social institutions by appealing to Nature with the assertion that men must eat, for hunger alone does not explain the diversity of economic systems. Nor can one reduce the great works of men to products of human institutions and associations. For example, society is not a "cause" of literature; it is only a condition under which writers work. Nor can one reduce the sciences to mere systematic figments of the imagination.

None of these three realms of study is reducible to any of the others, but the subject-matter fields of the humanities (e.g.,

2   "Humanities," *The Johns Hopkins Magazine,* May-June, 1960, 24.
3   Some of the ideas here and later in this chapter are indebted to Richard McKeon, "The Nature and Teaching of the Humanities," *Journal of General Education,* III (1949), 295.

literature, philosophy) are not reducible to operations performed in only one realm. These subject matters may have settled primarily in one realm, as literature has in the humanities, but they have sent colonists into the others. By this we mean that the complete study of any subject matter—literature, for example—may require operations that are scientific, operations that are humanistic, and operations characteristic of the social studies.

Suppose we are studying a work of science. Whether it is Harvey on the *Motions of the Blood* or a recent chemistry text does not matter. We would, in the first instance, deal with it scientifically, attempting to test its propositions against the evidence of nature. But the work has arisen in a specific social environment and will affect that environment and be affected by it. Further, the experiment is the expression of an individual and is stated in language and abstractions that may be judged according to standards for style and completeness in their use. These social and humanistic aspects of scientific works, though often neglected, are inescapably part of them.

One can, for example, almost go so far as to call certain styles in mathematics Chippendale or Italian Provincial, though this is a bit whimsical. But the life and work of the French mathematician Évariste Galois offer a case in point. Here is Romanticism at its most extreme. A contemporary illustration shows Galois with eyes dreaming off to the horizon and a pronounced Byronic sneer playing on his lips. Galois led a life as gaudy as Byron's, dying before he was twenty-one in a duel over a woman—a duel with sinister political overtones, for Galois was a revolutionary. Despite his tragically short life he left behind, as did the other great Romantic protagonists, permanent achievements. Among them were his demonstrations, in a paper revised on the eve of the fatal duel, that it is impossible to trisect an angle with ruler and compass alone, and that one cannot with complete accuracy solve equations of the fifth degree or over solely in terms of radicals. His essay is in the best Romantic style; the method of proof is characterized by intuitive leaps rather than by plodding rationalism. Certainly a poet like Wordsworth, who wrote that "We murder to dissect," would have been pleased by the limitations Galois placed on merely mechanical operations.

METHODS AND PRIORITIES OF STUDY

In any case, scientists indicate a humanistic concern when they speak of experiments as "clean" or of mathematical proofs as "elegant," as well as when they concern themselves with the effects of machines on man. Again, a novel may be examined as a work of art, but also as evidence of a social condition or as a statement about human nature. Similarly, social scientists first examine the qualities and uses of political institutions. But the historian Burckhardt can treat the Renaissance state as a work of art, and the philosopher Hobbes can discuss it as evidence for a view of human nature.

So we may examine great works scientifically or socially as well as humanistically. But we ought not to look three ways at once. Rather, we ought to observe priorities in the questions we ask, and we ought not to attach answers from one realm of study to questions proper to another. This last point must be emphasized because the recent prestige of science and social studies has sometimes forced their sort of answers on humanistic questions. The result has been a confusion in both questions and answers.

Perhaps an anecdote, half pedagogical fantasy, half actual occurrence, will explain this. Some time ago we visited the Treasury Room of the Cloisters, a museum of medieval arts and crafts in New York City. America has no Middle Ages, but evidently someone decided we needed one and, being American, he was able to buy it. Not just a single abbey or a shrine, but choice parts of several dozen. This is the Cloisters. The Treasury Room is a favorite in the museum. It has a more human scale than the others. On the walls hover carved saints with an earthbound, middle-class air. In a case a small brass dragon calmly swallows a small brass man. In a distant corner is a half-life-size sculpture in oak. The label reads "Madonna, Burgundian, XVth century." Our examination of this Madonna one afternoon was interrupted by the passing of other visitors. Since we are more scholar than gentleman, we eavesdropped. The first to comment on Madonna, Burgundian, XVth century, was one of two men in their late forties, both with well-cared-for, professional faces.

"Not much sense of anatomy there," he said.

"Hip-shot," said the other.

"Cart her off to the chiropractor."

They walked away. It was time to taxi downtown and sew a stomach.

Next to come by were a man and his wife, exemplars of the new American Gothic: middle-aged, middle-income, middle-western; serious tourists.

"Why did the paint peel off?" asked the wife.

"Something in the wood, maybe," was the reply, "Chemicals or maybe weather. I'll bet they could do it right nowadays. Too bad they didn't have the latex stuff we used on the porch."

Finally, there were two of what the late Helen Hokinson called "the Girls," briefly escaped from the suburbs and the struggle to marry off daughters. One of them sized up the Madonna in a somewhat irritated stare.

"I could never really live with it in the same room," she said. "I mean all this heavy Catholic stuff does the wrong thing to me. To tell you the truth, Gloria, I don't see how you brought yourself to vote for Kennedy."

Thereupon we had a snobbish vision of the great sculpture of the world with these six, endlessly multiplied, forever moving past. We wondered why the Madonna did not intercede on her own behalf. But there was no light, no lightning. The sins of bad criticism are too common to tempt divine interference; in matters of taste there must be dispute. So let us examine the blunders in the Treasury Room.

Rejoinder I: The Madonna as bad anatomy   The doctors were expressing a scientific criticism of a great work. But because they had not first examined the work humanistically, they made several mistakes. To begin with, they assumed that a great work can (without such prior examination) always be taken as direct evidence for the state of knowledge at the time it was created. The sculptor of the Madonna probably knew a great deal of anatomy—possibly little less than the doctors themselves. Certainly his own observation would have enabled him to recognize an abnormal relation of hips and spine. Had the doctors observed how the distortion of the hips made possible the calm expressiveness of the folds in the drapery and the strong volumes of the torso—had they begun with the analysis of the Madonna as a work of sculpture—they would have found a reason for the "bad anatomy" far more valid than the supposed ignorance of the sculptor. How ignorant of anatomy we may be thought when five centuries from now the critical descendants of such doctors discover paintings with two noses and three breasts! The second mistake the doctors made was their confusion of scientific with humanistic questions. Anatomically speaking, the Madonna is a false statement. But this is irrelevant to the fact that as a work of art it is a great statement. To confuse these two ways of looking at her is to reduce criticism to a vague and untenable standard of "realism" (mere copying) or to have no esthetic standards at all.

Rejoinder II: The Madonna as primitive technology
The serious couple were more accurate than the doctors in thinking that the sculptor of the Madonna knew less about the technology of paint than we do. But their failure (in addition to their failing to "see" the sculpture at all) was that they missed important questions to be asked about it, even about its paint. What was the statue like originally? Can we or ought we to "restore" it? If the parts of a work of art are significantly related to one another, what makes it possible for this work to maintain its integrity and effect although one of its parts, the polychrome, is almost completely gone? And, too, they accepted the specious notion that art improves with technology and, hence, that art exhibits Progress or "gets better" with time.

Rejoinder III: The Madonna as someone else's beliefs
We can be less sympathetic to the suburban matron because hers was a failure of heart as well as of mind. She correctly identified Catholicism as one of the institutional conditions under which the Burgundian Madonna was produced, and she also identified its now secondary use in ritual. But because she disliked Roman Catholicism, the dominant religion of the Middle Ages, she condemned a great work. She had reduced the work to a social thesis and had rejected it. If we were to follow her example, we should conclude by rejecting as bad every work that we ourselves had not produced and therefore could

not agree with. This would be nonsensical or would lead to an eccentric cult of modernity. Our matron would have been much better off had she treated the Madonna as a work of art. At least then her bias might have gone unexposed.

We cannot attempt to know a work with any thoroughness unless we apply all three kinds of analysis to it—humanistic, social, and scientific. But we must be scrupulous to take one view at a time, and we must heed priorities, viewing art first as art and only later as history or anatomy. Unless we proceed in this way, we may confuse important questions or miss them entirely. What is true of the Madonna is, of course, true of all objects of humanistic study, literary and philosophical works among them. We ought to begin, then, by examining such works humanistically. But precisely what would this involve? It would involve many operations, of which we can suggest only a few.

USES AND LIMITATIONS OF THE HUMANITIES

The humanities deal with the qualities of the great works of men and the relations among these qualities. Specifically, students of the humanities proceed by subjecting works to close reading or observation. They examine the adequacy of the expression to what is being expressed. They examine the possibilities of the medium of expression and how these possibilities are realized or neglected in a given work. Where the expression is obscure they attempt to clarify it by appealing to the history of language or of other media of expression and to custom and convention. Students of the humanities (especially in philosophy) also deal with the consistency and propriety of abstractions and with the use of symbols and ideas. They also deal with the forms of works and with the particular excellence proper to each form. But essentially they try to discover the nature of the great works of men and what makes particular works worthy of our praise.

The role of literature in promoting understanding   What are the uses of such studies? We are commonly told that the study of the humanities develops manners and morals, assures us of making correct decisions in everyday affairs, provides us with certain practical skills, and guarantees that we will lead what is called a "full" life. College catalogs are full of such incredible promises. Perhaps only the hardening effect of American advertising keeps students from crying fraud and suing for their tuition.

But for all their extremity there is something in the claims. The study of literature, for example, does increase our understanding of actual experience. An essential aspect of the form of great drama is, to use Bertrand Evans' term for it, "discrepant awareness." Throughout his book on *Shakespeare's Comedies* Evans shows how Shakespeare permits his audience an awareness of men and events greater than the awareness he permits the characters in his plays.[4] When Hamlet refrains from killing Claudius lest he send the praying murderer's soul to heaven, we know that Claudius cannot pray, though Hamlet does not know it. Our superior knowledge enables us to understand Hamlet as he does not understand himself, and to understand the irony of his attempt to take on himself decisions that belong only to heaven. From the larger structural features of Shakespeare's plays (the placing of scenes in this or that order) to the small details of texture (the use of this metaphor, of that word), the entire play is dedicated to the end that persons and events give up to the audience the profoundest secrets of their being.

Such is the form of drama. The form of individual experience, however, works against, not for, awareness. Crucial events drown in trivial distractions. Events, in turn, mask tendencies, and private associations flaw our understanding of both. Above all, self-interest and the instinct of self-preservation lead us to distort our experience. One of the prime uses of the humanities is their role in freeing us, however briefly, from the effects of self-interest and initiating us into disinterestedness. Through literature, for example, we enter a world different from the everyday, different not only because of its details but because in it we are neither forced nor tempted to respond defensively. The form of literature frames this imagined world, emphasizing its "esthetic distance" and directing our awareness to things as they actually are in their imagined contexts.

4   (New York: Oxford University Press, 1960).

As Marianne Moore puts it, poets are

> 'literalists of
> the imagination'—above
>   insolence and triviality [who] can present
> for inspection, 'imaginary gardens with real toads in
>   them.'[5]

The work of literature thus becomes a safe "arena" in which we may react to things as they are by undergoing symbolic experiences which neither threaten nor reward us, nor compel us to act.

The relations between literary study and other aspects of moral understanding have been clearly set forth by I. A. Richards in *Principles of Literary Criticism:*

> Instead of recognizing that value lies in the 'minute particulars' of response and attitude, we have tried to find it in conformity to abstract prescriptions and general rules of conduct. The artist is an expert in the 'minute particulars' and *qua* artist pays little or no attention to generalisations which he finds in actual practice are too crude to discriminate between what is valuable and the reverse. For this reason the moralist has always tended to distrust or to ignore him. Yet since the fine conduct of life springs only from fine ordering of responses far too subtle to be touched by any general ethical maxims, this neglect of art by the moralist has been tantamount to a disqualification. . . . Bad taste and crude responses are not mere flaws in an otherwise admirable person. They are actually a root evil from which other defects follow. No life can be excellent in which the elementary responses are disorganised and confused.[6]

The role of literature in promoting disinterestedness   In literary study we undertake the practice of disinterestedness and the perfection of a fidelity in response to "minute par-

5   Moore, pp. 40–41.
6   5th ed. (New York: Harcourt, Brace and World, 1934), pp. 61–62.

ticulars". In doing so, we attempt to duplicate under the most favorable circumstances what the writer himself has achieved with difficulty. For creation in literature, as in other fields, is not merely "expression." As T. S. Eliot put it in his essay on "Tradition and the Individual Talent":

> What happens [to the writer as he works] is a continual surrender of himself as he is at the moment to something more valuable. The progress of an artist is a continual self-sacrifice, a continual extinction of personality.[7]

In excellent works, what used to be called so pungently the author's "foul papers" record a drive toward "impersonality and concreteness, away from personal sentiment and autobiography." In inferior works, the revision sheets seem to show changes that are the results of impulse, with "the last version putting an end rather arbitrarily to an inherently endless succession of transformations."[8] What is true of the writer in writing is true of the reader in reading. The inferior reader interprets arbitrarily and without direction. The successful reader interprets away from his own concerns and sentiments and toward a concrete, impersonal response to the particulars of a work. Of course, neither reader nor writer can reach the goal of complete impersonality, for we can never wholly abandon our selves.

The limitations of the humanities   Yet common observation should convince us that while disinterested study of the humanities may, under favorable circumstances, lead to the intellectual virtues, it alone will not make us good or clever, or masters of our fate, or even masters of the English sentence. There is, after all, a difference between knowing and doing— and, even more important, a difference between knowledge and wisdom. King James I of England was reputed to be a good scholar, but his political ineptness led his contemporaries to

7 *Selected Essays, 1917–1932* (New York: Harcourt, Brace and World, 1932), pp. 6–7.

8 This and the quotation immediately preceding it are from Arnheim, Auden, Shapiro, and Stauffer, *Poets at Work* (New York: Harcourt, Brace and World, 1948), p. 54, p. 137. The first quotation is from Stauffer's interesting analysis of poetic revision, and the second from Arnheim's essay on the psychology of the poetic process.

call him the wisest fool in Christendom. Doctor Johnson, a great critic, had table manners that were a public nuisance. Socrates' marriage was supposed to have been extremely unhappy, and the author of a recent excellent work on ethics was convicted of a nasty petty crime.

This is not a catalog of freaks, but the common lot. Good economists are not always rich; good philosophers are not always happy or wise. Between knowledge and action there is a barrier we cannot wish or work away. It is not the barrier of ignorance, nor the barrier between what is and what ought to be. These we may breach a little. But we cannot breach the barrier of our natures. We may cultivate our talents, but we cannot exchange human nature for any other.

Perhaps this should be put in a less sad and cryptic way. It is obvious that knowledge and taste are related to morality and practical skills. But we cannot say that knowledge and taste inevitably make one good or successful. To believe this is to deny the possibility of morality, for it is to assume that in all circumstances men will react to a given experience in a precisely predictable way. This is to reduce men to machines by denying freedom of action and thus the possibility of moral choice. Moreover, such a belief is misleading. It can cause us to forget that the knowledge provided by the humanities is worth having for its own sake, as a delight. It is also both naïve and debasing to such knowledge to think of it only as a tool: naïve because we then underestimate the difficulty of acting morally and the difference between knowing and acting; and debasing because we then come to value only the knowledge that seems of use at the moment.

When it comes to being happy or good, we are in the situation of the man who hunts possum after dark. In order to hit the possum he must aim off-target. Perhaps humanistic knowledge will help make us good and successful. But not necessarily so. It is not easy to turn a reading of Homer into good deeds or cash. You have to be a Cecil B. DeMille to do it.

The ultimate uses of the humanities   But if they will not inevitably make us virtuous or happy, what, beyond their obvious role in promoting sensitivity and disinterest, is the use of studies such as literature? Their ultimate use is perhaps related to what keeps them from being immediately useful—

the barrier between knowledge and wisdom. That barrier is the mystery of the Self, a mystery not because like many other "problems" it is not yet "solved," but because it cannot *be* solved as other problems are. Other problems we can get outside of; we can see them as objects. But to examine the Self is to be both subject and object. "I cannot get outside my skin," said the philosopher Hume. "How can we know the dancer from the dance?" asked the poet Yeats. The mystery of the Self is the barrier between knowledge and wisdom, between knowing and knowing how to act.

Each of us, to the extent that he feels it at all, feels the loneliness of a self he cannot get outside of. To be told that this is a vertebrate self, or an organization self, or a consumer self is no solace. The sciences and the social studies can give us only partial images of man, images which are necessarily faceless and statistical, images in which we cannot see our own, images with which we cannot console ourselves. It is only the humanities that attempt whole images of man, unqualified and unreduced. Knowing these images we may say: Like St. Paul I am on this road; I have thought this with Plato; I sat on the edge of my bed and like Telemachus I wept that my father was not here. Only the humanities allow us glimpses of our unexchangeable selves, glimpses that we can contemplate without a certain discouragement and sense of limitation.

Let us put this another way. Any cat can pace off his territory on this planet. For fifty yards around the house this is his place; here he is at his ease; here he is confident. He sniffs these marigolds and knows they are his. He has been here before. Human beings have "lost" many of these animal instincts, the rhythms that unite this planet and its creatures. But we have not lost the need for our territory and our confidence. To study the great works of man is to find a territory and a confidence: to know that this is our place, that here we have left our mark. The universe may have its frightening blankness, but in such works, at least, we have put our collective signature on part of it.

Further, the image of man that emerges from the sciences and the social studies today is largely an image of man diminished: man the outcome of his genes, man the product of environments and institutions. This is the image of fabricated man. But from the humanities, from the study of the great works of

man, emerges another image: the image of *Homo Faber,* Man
the Maker. Especially now do we need this image, when social
forces seem to reduce man to a pawn, and technology seems to
create much better pawns than he. In this age of blind Force
it is well to contemplate the great works of man. For if man has
worked with complex and recalcitrant materials to create his
arts and systems of thought, why can he not create even more
grandly in their kind? If the *Odyssey,* why not the pleasing city?
If the Platonic dialogues, why not the rational civilization? The
barriers between thought and action, between knowledge and
wisdom, will remain, but an appreciation of the humane
achievements will maintain our spirits for the attempt to leap
those barriers. This is what we mean when we assign to the
humanities the uses of giving us a home in the universe and a
confidence in human possibilities.

   But to some, a fortunate some, all this is irrelevant. In the
humanities they will find nothing less than a personal identity.
We are thinking now of those who were collecting words and
shapes and notions when they collected stones or dolls. For them
such "uses" as we have cited will seem useless. When Philo-
cosmos has said to them, as he does in Samuel Daniel's poem
Mvsophilvs: Containing a generall Defence of Learning:

> Fond man Musophilus, that thus dost spend
> In an vngainefull arte thy deerest daies,
> Tyring thy wits, and toiling to no end,
> But to attaine that idle smoake of Praise;
> Now when this busie world cannot attend
> Th'vntimely musicke of neglected layes.
> Other delights then these, other desires
> This wiser profit-seeking age requires.

they will reply, as did Musophilus:

> This is the thing that I was borne to do,
> This is my Scene, this part must I fulfill.[9]

For some students, their studies in the humanities—in literature, in the arts, in philosophy—will be like flight to a bird,
that settling of the soul into its natural condition which some
philosophers call happiness.

9   *Poems and a Defence of Ryme,* ed. A. C. Sprague (Cambridge, Mass.: Harvard
University Press, 1930), pp. 69, 85.

Chapter Two **P** *The Language of Poetry*

oetry uses, in a deliberate, formalized way, those devices of language in which we find a natural enjoyment. Poetic language differs from other kinds of language not by greater profundity but by the degree to which it depends for its effect upon the organization of various elements, among which rhythm and sound are especially evident. Of even greater ultimate importance, however, are the imagistic and figurative elements of poetic language. These give to poetry a particularity and a richness of expression that distinguish it from the abstractness of philosophical discourse and the emotional neutrality of scientific statement. Because of its special emphasis upon the *means* of expression, poetry requires from the reader, more than anything else, a concern with and a sensitivity to the resources of language.

IT FORCES ITS ATTENTIONS UPON US

If there is anything that an instructor may be sure most of his students already know about poetry, it is that they dislike it. For too many of us, "poetry" is associated with unwilling memorization and witless recitation, with the painful sentimentality printed in greeting cards or embroidered on satin cushions, or with an obscurity whose only appeal is to snobbery. Thereby convinced that all poems must be dull, namby-pamby, or inaccessible, students often conclude that the only decent thing is to ignore poetry or, if degree requirements prevent this, to refuse to enjoy it.

Yet in spite of such familiar prejudices, poetry, or at any rate the poetic use of language, is more genuinely a part of us than we know. Even the person who complains boastfully that he cannot understand poetry has nonetheless set some of his own life to its very measure. For, as Samuel Taylor Coleridge said, poetry is language that calls attention to itself; and who has not, in some way or other, often taken delight in the antics language can perform? At least when we were children we often found such delight; the attention-getting devices of language that are the stuff of poetry provide a kind of accompaniment to childhood. Rhymes fascinated us, especially when we discovered how they could be used to characterize our friends—or enemies: "Silly Billy!" "Jane, Jane, gives me a pain!" "Baby Ned wets the bed!" Alliteration also had its particular joys, as in those famous tongue twisters, "Peter Piper picked a peck of pickled peppers" and "Big boys bottle the blue bug's blood." As children we also explored the rich world of simile and metaphor: "Batter, you swing like a rusty gate!" "Who's the butter ball playing second base?" Puns and a variety of verbal jokes enlivened our days, even if they were not always the kind one could repeat to his parents or Sunday School teacher. And constantly the rhythm of language lent its special bewitching authority to childhood's fun, as in

> One potato, two potato, three potato, four;
> Five potato, six potato, seven potato—MORE!

and in the infinite variety of playground taunts that fit, as if by magic, a single unmistakable cadence:

Nya   nya nya   nya   NYAAAA   nya

Jimmy's got a G I R L-friend!

I know something Y O U don't!

Bill's the teacher's P E-et!

Nursery rhymes, word games, jingles, and the like offer endless examples of the ways language has given us pleasure by calling attention to itself. Only the most hopelessly solemn adult could conclude from such illustrations that poetry, insofar as it both derives from and provides this kind of enjoyment, is merely a childish aberration. A more just conclusion would be that precisely because poetry is rooted in this primitive pleasure—a pleasure to which no one is fully a stranger—its essential place is not on the periphery but at the very center of our most distinctly human involvement: our involvement with the possibilities of language.

WE FOCUS OUR ATTENTION UPON IT

A further advantage in approaching the subject of poetic language through a consideration of its most familiar and simple instances is that their very simplicity makes it easy to demonstrate in detail some of the ways such language works; and if our appreciation of any art is to develop at all, we need to become more conscious of the possibilities for manipulation, organization, and expression that its medium offers. We need, in short, to know what it means to be "artistic" in that particular field. With this need in mind let us look carefully at another of these childish jingles, a well-known nursery rhyme:

"To bed, to bed," said Sleepy Head.
"Tarry awhile," said Slow.
"Put on the pan," said Greedy Nan,
"We'll sup before we go."

This little verse is not, of course, as important or meaningful as, let us say, a good newspaper editorial. However, it *is* more of a poem; and since it is "the language of poetry" that we are considering, not "the wisdom of poetry," it is all the better if our example insures us against the distractions of profundity.

Notice first how important, as well as how obvious, the structure of the poem is. As so many objects do, this poem depends for its effect upon its use of the magic number three. There is a German proverb that says "All good things come in three," and we need not appeal to the arcane "science" of numerology to realize how true this is, especially in the organization of language: "Friends, Romans, countrymen"; Tom, Dick, and Harry; "blood, sweat, and tears." This last, incidentally, Churchill originally intoned as "blood, toil, tears, and sweat"; but even his masterful sense of phrase has yielded before the seemingly irresistible triad. Perhaps the power of three somehow to suggest rhetorical and dramatic inclusiveness gives it, as a basis of verbal organization, something of the same "resistance to stress" that distinguishes the triangle as a principle in architecture. In any case, what we have in the nursery rhyme is a situation composed of three opposing elements. Quite simply, three persons wanting three different things. But any magic in the number three can hardly operate without a degree of verbal arrangement, and that is where the poetry comes in. Suppose you had read:

> Sleepy urged us to go to bed. On the other hand, Slow said, "What's the rush?" Then Greedy Nan had the idea that we ought to eat a bedtime snack.

It is still the same situation, apparently, but the life has gone out of it. In fact, even the effect of "threeness" is weakened, because the three characters are not individualized as they were in the poetic version. Clearly, no real poem is reducible to a mere paraphrase of its contents.

In the nursery rhyme itself, however, there is an unmistakable vividness. Each character is distinctly realized, and in the contrast among all three we have a sort of miniature drama.

> "To bed, to bed," said Sleepy Head.

There is urgency—we might even say the exasperation of fatigue—in the repetition of *To bed* and especially in the triple rhyme of which that phrase is a part. The strong iambic rhythm completes this precipitous effect, and the explosiveness of the *t, b,* and *d* sounds suggests Sleepy Head's frustrated efforts to jerk or prod the others into calling it quits for the night.

What a change comes over the poem as Slow is introduced to us in the languid second line! The marked iambic meter of the first line (that is, a pattern of unstressed followed by stressed syllables: da-DUM, da-DUM, da-DUM, da-DUM) with all its urgency is brought up short by the first foot of the second line, which is a trochee, just the reverse of iambic (DA-dum: TAR-ry). After the word *tarry*—which actually makes the poem do just that—the meter restores itself to the basic iambic, but the pace has slackened:

> "Tarry awhile," said Slow.

You notice too that instead of a staccato triple rhyme as in the first line, there are no rhymes at all as Slow's line meanders to its end. It has one foot less than line one, but the retarded tempo makes it seem at least as long.

Greedy Nan's part in the poem requires two lines. This is appropriate on several counts. The dynamics of the triple pattern often seem to require a resolution or the added complexity of "four against three." The alternating line lengths of tetrameter/trimeter reflect this four-three interplay. It is as if there were some rhythmic law requiring every *Eeny, Meeny,* and *Miny* to have a *Moe,* whether they want him or not. And Greedy Nan deserves half of this four-line poem because she is, in one sense, the synthesis of Sleepy Head and Slow. She argues for delay, like Slow, but with much of the forceful insistency of Sleepy Head:

> "Put on the pan," said Greedy Nan,
> "We'll sup before we go."

The first of these lines, with its internal rhyme, is like Sleepy Head's part of the poem; but the last line, which again has no internal rhyme, does form an end-rhyme with *Slow* (line two). Finally, there is no mistaking the effect of that wonderful word *sup,* with the natural dramatic pause that follows it. Could any word more clearly represent, in its sound and associations, the venial yet quintessential greediness of Greedy Nan?

The collective result of such features as we have been discussing is that they give the little nursery rhyme a remarkable completeness. That is another thing the language of poetry tries to do: to set the poem off as a kind of little world, a totality to which we would add nothing and from which we do not wish to remove anything. This quality becomes evident if one considers how thoroughly the nursery rhyme satisfies us of the *un*importance of such questions as: Exactly where *are* Sleepy Head, Slow, and Greedy Nan? Are those really their names? How old are they? What happens next? What does Greedy Nan want to put into that pan? Do they disagree like this every night? Is there a moral in this? What is the point of it all, anyway? These questions are unimportant because there is nothing in the poem that makes us expect an answer and nothing that provides one. They do not belong to the completeness of the poem; they are "brought in from outside." Of course other poems may legitimately raise such questions, but these other poems have their own laws of existence; they are their own separate worlds. As for the little rhyme we are considering, its completeness is one of distillation, not accumulation. In it we merely encounter, in a brief dramatic moment, a Sleepy Head, a Slow, and a Greedy Nan, unencumbered by either circumstantiality or abstract "significance."

VERSE, POETRY, AND PROSE – SOME DISTINCTIONS

Thus far our examination of the language of poetry has tended to stress the uses of sound and meter. It is natural to begin with these, because, for most of us, to speak of poetry is to speak of "verse," or that form of language which is distinguished from prose by its systematic employment of the effects of rhythm and sound. However, it can hardly be said that the terms *verse* and *poetry* are interchangeable. Everyone can think of certain *verses* that do not deserve to be called *poems*, and surely there are works in which sound and rhythm count for very little and yet for which the designation "poem" seems quite appropriate. On the other hand, a very broad definition—based upon the original Greek meaning of *poem* as a made thing—would not ordinarily be useful if it required us to consider all novels, stories, and plays (or even works of history) as *poems*. In view of such difficulties, an idea of poetry like the one cited earlier from Coleridge seems especially sound. If we may regard poetry as language that calls attention to itself, it is clear that patterns of rhythm and sound are by no means the only elements of language that make it "poetic."

Before going on to discuss some of these other elements, let us consider briefly a much more complicated distinction than the one between poetry and verse: that between poetry and prose. Here again the notion we have borrowed from Coleridge provides valuable insight. To say that in poetry the language calls attention to itself is to suggest that, in the poem, language is not merely the *means* by which the writer expresses his object, as in prose; the language is *itself* an object. More simply, we "see through" prose, but we "look at" poetry.

To put the matter in this way is, of course, to remind ourselves of the artificiality of the distinction. No poem is totally "opaque"; for, words being what they are, a coherent construct of language is almost sure to be "about" something. Nor is any work of prose so "transparent" that it achieves expression absolutely free of any sense of the linguistic medium or even of stylistic contrivance. At one extreme, then, we find poetry of the densest and most intricate sort—examples of which, incidentally, come from all literary eras. The opposite extreme we could assign to both the randomness of everyday conversation on the one hand and the prefabricated quality of standard journalistic style on the other. But there is an area where poetry and prose shade into one another; for some pieces of prose are genuinely poetic, whereas some poems, or parts of poems, seem hardly poetic at all. Perhaps one had better be content to say simply that poems tend to make more use of "poetry" than prose does.

IMAGES AND FIGURES OF SPEECH—
THE CONCRETE AND THE ANALOGICAL IN POETRY

Of the many features of language which may constitute this poetic quality, the two most important are undoubtedly its *imagistic* and its *figurative* elements. It has been said that poetry pushes language in two directions. One is toward sensuous particularity, toward directly rendering in words the world of eye and ear and touch. The other is toward figuration—that is, the oblique form of discourse that seeks to convey one world by comparing it with another.[1] It should be added that poetry often

---

1   René Wellek and Austin Warren, *Theory of Literature* (New York: Harcourt, Brace and World, 1949), p. 190.

pushes language in these two directions at the same time; however, it is convenient to consider them separately.

Imagery—the appeal to the senses   The movement of poetry toward sensuous particularity by means of imagery distinguishes it from such other uses of language as the scientific and the philosophical. It is a common enough observation that science and philosophy concern themselves with abstractions— that is, with concepts, laws, and other forms of generalization that are detached, or at least detachable, from particular instances. Poetry, on the other hand, usually has a greater stake in the realm of the particular, the concrete. "Poetry . . . is not so fine a thing as philosophy," Keats once generously wrote, "for the same reason that an eagle is not so fine a thing as a truth." But as most poets know—certainly Keats among them— a poetry that does not fill the mind with images of the real world can seldom redeem itself, even by its philosophy. So true is this that a recent critic has been led to wonder whether a Platonist could ever be a poet. At any rate, a poem probably ought not to become so concerned with the ideal that it neglects the actual. Carl Sandburg both spoke to this point and illustrated it when he described poetry as the synthesis of hyacinths and biscuits.

"Logicians may reason about abstractions," wrote Thomas Babington Macaulay, that champion of plain sense, "but the great mass of men must have images." Poetic language commonly makes use of the fact that our minds often respond more strongly, and more richly, to an image than to a proposition. Therefore, the most vivid and moving effects of a poem are likely to be the result of the quality of its images rather than of its explicit statements. Let us look at three stanzas of Tennyson's poem "Mariana" by way of example:

> With blackest moss the flower-plots
> Were thickly crusted, one and all;
> The rusted nails fell from the knots
> That held the pear to the gable-wall.
> The broken sheds look'd sad and strange:
> Unlifted was the clinking latch;
> Weeded and worn the ancient thatch

Upon the lonely moated grange.
　　She only said, "My life is dreary,
　　　He cometh not," she said;
　　She said, "I am aweary, aweary,
　　　I would that I were dead!"

. . . .

All day within the dreamy house
　The doors upon their hinges creak'd;
The blue fly sung in the pane; the mouse
　Behind the mouldering wainscot shriek'd,
Or from the crevice peer'd about.
　Old faces glimmer'd thro' the doors,
　Old footsteps trod the upper floors,
Old voices called her from without.
　　She only said, "My life is dreary,
　　　He cometh not," she said;
　　She said, "I am aweary, aweary,
　　　I would that I were dead!"

The sparrow's chirrup on the roof,
　The slow clock ticking, and the sound
Which to the wooing wind aloof
　The poplar made, did all confound
Her sense; but most she loathed the hour
　When the thick-moted sunbeam lay
　Athwart the chambers, and the day
Was sloping toward his western bower.
　　Then said she, "I am very dreary,
　　　He will not come," she said;
　　She wept, "I am aweary, aweary,
　　　O God, that I were dead!"

Each of these stanzas is made up of several lines of objective description followed by a refrain wherein the lady expresses her despair. The refrain is important, of course, in
revealing to us the situation; it tells us that a lady waits weari-
somely and with waning hope for her lover's return. But certainly it is the imagery of the descriptive passages that generates
the poem's mood, that conveys to us not merely the *fact* of the

lady's desolation but its *quality,* its very flavor. The lady tells us that she is weary and that she wishes she were dead, and in view of the scene in which the poet has placed her it would be strange indeed if she felt otherwise. But of course the scene is not so much a cause of her depression as its objective equivalent. The rusted nails falling from the knots, the broken sheds, the slow ticking of the clock all suggest the dreary passing of time—time that wears away without fulfillment. Other images add to this extraordinary rendering of internal desolation. Small sounds that only deepen the human silence echo the emptiness of hopeless existence: the creak of doors, the buzz of flies, the chirp of a sparrow, the moaning of the wind. And what can one say concerning the concluding detail of that shaft of late afternoon sun, "thick-moted," striking across the drab chamber, except to mark it as the finishing touch to the picture of utter vacancy and tedium?

The poet has made few assertions about these images, and in fact the connection between the "physical exterior" and the "emotional interior" is never explicitly drawn. Nevertheless, the descriptive details are sufficiently vivid in themselves to command the proper response and to make their relevance to the heroine's state of mind unmistakable. Indeed, if it were not for the emotional appeal of the poem's imagery, the forsaken lady's anguished refrain would seem no more than a melodramatic commonplace.

Figuration as qualitative expression As we shift our attention from the image-making to the analogy-forming aspects of poetry, we must not overlook the fact that a grasp of figurative language, no less than an appreciation of sensory imagery for its own sake, demands a keen respect for the *concrete*. As an illustration (the fact that it is taken from a work of prose is immaterial), consider the words of Don Quixote:

"How blind is he who cannot see through a sieve!"

Although it is obvious that this exclamation cannot merely be taken literally, that Cervantes' hero is speaking parabolically, we have first to give our minds to the literal situation in order to understand what it is intended to express. That is, we must recall that there are two ways of looking into a sieve: by focusing one's vision at the wires, or by focusing in such a way as to look, *through* the wires, at whatever is beyond. The perfectly elementary optical phenomenon which causes the sieve to appear opaque in the first instance but to seem transparent in the second expresses, metaphorically, alternative ways of regarding physical reality. What Don Quixote is saying, our comprehension of the homely sieve image shows us, is that to look only at the surface of phenomenal reality is a kind of blindness; true vision involves a perception of what lies beyond.

It should thus be apparent that figurative language, far from neglecting actuality, does in fact demand from us a considerable sensitivity to it; nevertheless, it seems to be the case that no aspect of poetry suffers more distrust—perhaps even contempt—from realistic and tidy minds than its disturbing habit of saying one thing and meaning something else. It is often felt that poetry is vague and inexact compared to other kinds of discourse, especially scientific discourse, which are precise and accurate and reliable. Even disregarding the fact that many of the classic statements of science are couched in metaphor, it is necessary to modify this common conception of the virtues of a scientific language, which *measures*, as compared to a poetic language, which *evokes*. It is certainly fair to say that scientific language is precise when it deals chiefly in *quantities*—when it attempts to say how much, how fast, how heavy, or how often. But it is less successful in giving an adequate account of quality. In qualitative matters scientific language may often be quite imprecise, for the apprehension of quality requires the kind of appeal to the familiar or the simple experience as the route to knowledge of the unfamiliar or the complex experience that is the special power of figurative statement. "This year's Miss Universe measures 36–23–36" is a scientific statement of sorts, and it is a measure of our own imaginative poverty that these statistics do represent for us a shadowy image of the ideal. For Miss Universe—if she is real at all—must be more than a silhouette. Her beauty must have *qualities* as well as dimensions, and to express these qualities requires another kind of language. Not the language of press agents: *ravishing, exotic, provocative*—such threadbare adjectives have no precision in this context. That is, they define nothing accurately; however, poetry *does*, when it

comes to assessing the quality of human beauty and expressing
it figuratively:

> There is a garden in her face,
> Where roses and white lilies grow.

> She was a phantom of delight

> My clumsiest dear, whose hands shipwreck vases[2]

> No spring nor summer beauty hath such grace
> As I have seen in one autumnal face.

There are a great many kinds of figures of speech, but by
all odds the most important to poetry is metaphor. (In this connection, we take the liberty of using the term metaphor somewhat broadly to include *similes,* in which comparison is made
explicit by the use of *as* or *like.*) Metaphor, one eminent critic
has said, is the basic formal principle of poetry, just as myth is
basic to fiction. It is certainly true that without an ability to
understand metaphor and to respond to its effectiveness no one
can hope to make much out of poetry. The subject of figurative
language in general and metaphor in particular is too complicated to discuss fully in a brief chapter, but another example
may help indicate why a grasp of metaphor is probably the
main key to understanding poetry and why a poet can often say
more through the use of metaphor than he can by literal statement. The poem we are using for this purpose is so short that
there is very little more to it than a single metaphor.

MEMORY

> One had a lovely face,
> And two or three had charm,
> But charm and face were in vain
> Because the mountain grass

2   From *The Iron Pastoral* by John Frederick Nims (New York: William Sloane
Associates, 1947), p. 82.

Cannot but keep the form
Where the mountain hare has lain.

——*W. B. Yeats*[3]

Now here is a poem which, read literally, makes no sense at all. What in the world, we may ask, do the properties of mountain grass have to do with charm and face being in vain? What is the logic of the statement the poem makes? It is at this point, one suspects, that many students either wash their hands of the poem or begin to indulge in free association. Yet, on the metaphoric level, the poem is clear enough, though the metaphor *is* a rather strange one.

The poem, we gather from its title, has to do with memory; and we discover that the image presented in the last three lines—the image of the grass retaining the impression of the wild rabbit that has nestled in it—is a metaphoric expression of the way memory retains the form (that is, the impression, the recollection) of some object long after that object has ceased to be physically present. Then we see that *charm* and *face*—whatever they refer to—were unable to efface or supplant this remembrance. At about this point in our examination of the poem, we ought to begin to see what it is about. The subject is, of course, common enough in poetry: the speaker's memory of a lost love persists despite a series of intervening encounters with other women. He admits that these other women—some of them, at least—had certain attractions: one had a lovely face and two or three had charm. But charm and face—the superficial attraction of personality and physical appearance respectively—simply could not take the place of an earlier love and thus blot *her* from his memory.

However, if we think carefully about the metaphor in the poem, its meaning is much more subtle than this account of it suggests. The image which stands in the poem for *memory* is a depression in the grass where a hare *has* lain, since what the mind holds is not the object *itself* but only the *mark* of the object.

A sense of loss is hardly the same as the recovery of the thing lost. Thus the poem reveals with remarkable accuracy that painfully ironic power of memory, not to restore to us what we lose, but to remind us vividly of what is unrecapturable.

In considering the metaphor in this fashion, we are no longer merely addressing ourselves to the question, "What does it mean?" We are also asking, "What is its effect?" What does this metaphor express that literal statement could not express as well? What is its particular appropriateness in conveying the idea?

These questions suggest dimensions of understanding that have to do less with the reader's ability merely to fathom the literal sense of figurative statement than with his capacity to respond to its range of implications and to discern as precisely as possible the relation between the idea and the image that embodies it. One dimension of understanding, for example, requires a recognition that the similarities upon which the poem's metaphor depends are surely not sensory. That is to say, if we demand some physical analogy between the poet's mind and mountain grass, or between his beloved and a rabbit, the effect is ludicrous. But we should remind ourselves that the analogical basis of a metaphor is not always a physical similarity. In the case of this poem, it is a kind of emotional equivalence. In this connection it is important to notice that the grass is *mountain* grass and that the animal is a *mountain* hare. Both grass and hare, we see, are indigenous and wild, and, what is more, they belong to each other in a special way; consequently, we transfer our reactions to these qualities to the conception that the images figuratively represent. Then too, we should mark the effect of the image of an abandoned place where a creature once sought refuge and whose very outline the place still retains. A sensitive reader ought to find a genuine poignancy in such an image, a poignancy we naturally attach to the empty nest where life has been. In short, Yeats' metaphor demands an alertness of both mind and feeling if we hope to understand it well and respond to it fairly.

If nothing else, a poem such as this illustrates one of the fundamental functions of figurative language: it enables the poet to express himself more richly and more forcefully than he could by other means. But the power of such language does not end with self-expression; poetry is, for the skilled poet, a method of thought, and so it becomes, to the fit reader, a means of knowledge. A lover's sorrow is an ancient theme; nothing new, we may be sure, can be said on the subject. It is not, however, the novelty of the situation that Yeats' poem is about, but rather what that situation actually feels like. The speaker of the poem has not merely said, "I'm sad," nor has he simply moaned with grief. Neither of these forms of expression would communicate the emotion very distinctly or interest us very much. More than that, however, neither can—as the poem does—enhance our knowledge by enlarging and clarifying our experience.

APPRECIATIVE INSPECTION OR INCURIOUS ADVOCACY?

This discussion of poetic language began with the assumption that many people who dislike poetry do so largely because of mistaken ideas about it; it must conclude with the admission that some of those who say they like poetry are equally misguided. These are the ones who warn that poems lose their magic if they are examined with too much care, that the beauty of poetry withers beneath the glare of scrutiny. This attitude is often no more than an excuse for lazy-mindedness, and it makes impossible a genuine enjoyment of poetry. At least so it would seem if there is any truth in the Coleridgean dictum we have taken as a point of departure: that in poetry the language calls attention to itself. Surely the attentiveness which such language invites implies analysis and judgment. Hence, no one need feel that by reading closely he is violating the poet's creative privacy. The name *poet*, we remember, means "maker," and like any craftsman his pride is in his handiwork. We treat it according to its nature when we regard it as *art;* it is for us to study and admire.

Chapter Three

W

hat distinguishes lit-
erature from nonliterature is its invented quality.[1] What distinguishes fiction from nonfiction therefore is style, not subject
matter. Style is the way a writer writes, whatever he writes
about and regardless of its relationship to actual fact. It is, however, neither mere mannerism nor idiosyncrasy, but the sum of
those devices, inherited or newly invented, by which language
in its various possibilities is employed to bring an implied reader
into a hypothetical world, contrived by an empirical author,
speaking through an artificial voice.

By means of the distance these devices permit him to take,
the writer makes an object from the raw materials of subject
matter and the everyday use of language, as distinguished from
its esthetic use. The meaning, then, of a work of fiction can be
located at approximately the point where the reader perceives
in the work the relationship between style and subject matter,
as if these components were inseparable parts of one organism.

THE MATERIALS OF FICTION

Style is not simply those obvious ways in which one writer's
prose differs from another's or from everyone else's. If this were
the case, a student's unfortunate habit of misspelling a particu-

---

1   In the essays of Lamb, for example, the voice speaking to the reader is
not Lamb's, but that of an invented character, a persona. In this sense, Lamb's
essays may be said to be "fictional," that is, like fiction. Most contemporary
magazine articles lack this quality and are only articles, but Lamb's essays,
with their invented quality, are literature. All that goes into the invention
may be termed *style*.

lar word or his obsessive use of a certain adjective (the first is idiosyncratic; the second, manneristic) would be deemed "style." (In fact, *un-style* would be more appropriate, if we see in this student's writing a poverty of craftsmanship.) Moreover, fiction, that which is distinguished from nonfiction by style or invention, may be wholly "made up" or based partly on "what really happened yesterday in Chicago," but our right to call a book a work of fiction does not depend on determining whether it is mostly "truth" or mostly "made-up"—this task can be left to private detectives. It depends rather on how much of the writer's craft is evident and on whether our discernment of this craft leads us to what the book might mean.

The writer of fiction makes something which is like life; it is lifelike the way a tree is lifelike. One part seems to grow out of another, and its whole has, therefore, a logic and an integrity which is true—its own truth. Whether a writer uses "real life" materials or "makes them up," he invents something which exists finally independent of himself. This is why we say that a writer's enterprise is "esthetic," at a distance from his materials and himself. He imagines the kind of person who will read his book, and he directs his voice, often disguised, to this imagined reader. He transforms the materials of the everyday world—a world in which design or pattern or order is difficult to find— and imposes a discernible order on it. Finally, in the ways in which he brings the reader into the world which he has invented, the writer converts himself into a kind of fictional personage, an implied author. The character of the author is imagined by the reader, no less than his invented world is imagined by the author. Few of us knew Ernest Hemingway personally. Yet everyone who reads his work has a sense of a quality of mind behind and within his fiction which was, is, and will be (despite Hemingway's death) the quality of the implied author.

In an article written for the magazine *Commentary,* the American novelist Philip Roth began his discourse on the subject "Writing American Fiction" with the following narration. Our concern here is both with what Mr. Roth says and with the way he says it:[2]

Several winters back, while I was living in Chicago, the city was shocked and mystified by the death of two teen-age girls. So far as I know the populace is mystified still; as for the shock, Chicago is Chicago, and one week's dismemberment fades into the next's. The victims this particular year were sisters. They went off one December night to see an Elvis Presley movie, for the sixth or seventh time we are told, and never came home. Ten days passed and fifteen and twenty, and then the whole bleak city, every street and alley, was being searched for the missing Grimes girls, Pattie and Babs. A girl friend had seen them at the movie, a group of boys had had a glimpse of them afterwards getting into a black Buick; another group said a green Chevy, and so on and so forth, until one day the snow melted and the unclothed bodies of the two girls were discovered in a roadside ditch in a forest preserve on the West Side of Chicago. The coroner said he didn't know the cause of death and then the newspapers took over. One paper, I forget which one, ran a drawing of the girls on the back page, in bobby socks and levis and babushkas: Pattie and Babs a foot tall, and in four colors, like Dixie Dugan on Sundays. The mother of the two girls wept herself right into the arms of a local newspaper lady, who apparently set up her typewriter on the Grimes's front porch and turned out a column a day, telling us that these had been good girls, hardworking girls, average girls, churchgoing girls, et cetera. Late in the evening one could watch television interviews featuring schoolmates and friends of the Grimes sisters: the teen-age girls look around, dying to giggle; the boys stiffen in their leather jackets. "Yeah, I knew Babs, yeah, she was all right, yeah, she was popular. . . ." On and on until at last comes a confession. A Skid Row bum of thirty-five or so, a dishwasher, a prowler, a no-good named Benny Bedwell, admits to killing both girls, after he and a pal had cohabited with them for several weeks in various flea-bitten hotels. Hearing the news, the mother weeps and cries and tells the newspaper lady that the man is a liar—her girls, she insists now, were murdered the night they went off to the movie. The coroner continues to maintain (with rumblings from the press) that the girls show no signs of having had sexual intercourse. Meanwhile, everybody in Chicago is buying four papers a day, and Benny Bedwell, having supplied the police with an hour-by-hour chronicle of his adventures, is tossed in jail. Two nuns, teachers of the girls at the

2 From *Commentary,* March and September 1961, 31: 223–233; 32: 250–252. Copyright by the American Jewish Committee.

school they attended, are sought out by the newspapermen. They are surrounded and questioned and finally one of the sisters explains all. "They were not exceptional girls," the sister says, "they had no hobbies." About this time, some good-natured soul digs up Mrs. Bedwell, Benny's mother, and a meeting is arranged between this old woman and the mother of the slain teen-agers. Their picture is taken together, two overweight, overworked American ladies, quite befuddled but sitting up straight for the photographers. Mrs. Bedwell apologizes for her Benny. She says, "I never thought any boy of mine would do a thing like that." Two weeks later, or maybe three, her boy is out on bail, sporting several lawyers and a new one-button roll suit. He is driven in a pink Cadillac to an out-of-town motel where he holds a press conference. Yes—he barely articulates —he is the victim of police brutality. No, he is not a murderer; a degenerate maybe, but even that is going out the window. He is changing his life—he is going to become a carpenter (a carpenter!) for the Salvation Army, his lawyers say. Immediately, Benny is asked to sing (he plays the guitar) in a Chicago night spot for two thousand a week, or is it ten thousand? I forget. What I remember is that suddenly there is a thought that comes flashing into the mind of the spectator, or newspaper reader: is this all Public Relations? But of course not—two girls are dead. At any rate, a song begins to catch on in Chicago, "The Benny Bedwell Blues." Another newspaper launches a weekly contest: "How Do You Think the Grimes Girls Were Murdered?" and a prize is given for the best answer (in the opinion of the judges). And now the money begins; donations, hundreds of them, start pouring in to Mrs. Grimes from all over the city and the state. For what? From whom? Most contributions are anonymous. Just money, thousands and thousands of dollars—the *Sun-Times* keeps us informed of the grand total. Ten thousand, twelve thousand, fifteen thousand. Mrs. Grimes sets about refinishing and redecorating her house. A strange man steps forward, by the name of Shultz or Schwartz—I don't really remember, but he is in the appliance business and he presents Mrs. Grimes with a whole new kitchen. Mrs. Grimes, beside herself with appreciation and joy, turns to her surviving daughter and says, "Imagine me in that kitchen!" Finally the poor woman goes out and buys two parakeets (or maybe another Mr. Shultz presented them as a gift); one parakeet she calls "Babs," the other, "Pattie." At just about this point, Benny Bedwell, doubtless having barely learned to hammer a nail in straight, is extradited to Florida on the charge of having raped a twelve-year-old girl there. Shortly thereafter I left Chicago myself, and so far as I know, though Mrs. Grimes hasn't her two girls, she has a brand new dishwasher and two small birds.

THE PROVINCE OF FICTION

Mr. Roth then asks, "And what is the moral of so long a story? Simply this," he says, "that the American writer in the middle of the 20th century has his hands full in trying to understand, and then describe, and then make *credible* much of the American reality. It stupifies, it sickens, it infuriates, and finally it is even a kind of an embarrassment to one's own meager imagination. The actuality," he says, "is continually outdoing our talents, and the culture tosses up figures almost daily that are the envy of any novelist. Who, for example, could have invented Charles Van Doren?"

Let us concede, first of all, that Mr. Roth has a right to be sickened and infuriated by such raw material. Where is it written that writers should have stronger stomachs than other people? But that he is stupified by contemporary American life, that he understands it poorly should not surprise him much. He is an artist, a very good one, we think; but he is not a systematic philosopher, nor a cultural anthropologist. For him, precisely because he is an artist, the world must be a place of infinite wonder. He must think marvelous what others take for granted. When Dylan Thomas wrote: "The ball I threw while playing in the park/Has not yet reached the ground," he was expressing such wonder in a metaphor from childhood. And when Mr. Roth laments that his "meager talents" are an embarrassment in the face of material which seems beyond the imagination of the contemporary writer, material which seems to write its awful self, he is voicing a familiar complaint and is being, judging from his own work, needlessly modest. In fact, he is not talking about fiction at all, but is, instead, indulging in rather commonplace social criticism. There is evidence in the *Iliad*, for instance, that Homer did not think of war as an unmitigated blessing. As part of the Greek myth it was available as material for fiction. And there are scenes in the works of Dostoevsky which are both wildly fantastic and entirely believable at one and the same time, although it is probable that urban Russia was at least as sickening and infuriating and as stupifying to Dostoevsky in his time as Chicago is to the fiction writer today.

The point is that there is the second and the third and the fourth and the fifth thing about a work of fiction, but before that, there is the *first* thing, which Mr. Roth pretends for the sake of his argument not to know; namely, that literature is artificial—it is made up; that literature is one thing and that life, which is only the unstyled *subject matter* of literature, is something else altogether. The fiction writer *always,* if only intuitively, knows this, which is why he writes novels and not "page one" accounts of three-alarm fires. He knows this even when he writes articles asserting that American life is too bizarre for words. He knows there are ways and means of making the incredibly real seem credibly true, just as there are ways of making the incredibly true seem credibly real. He can do this by traditional means, or he can invent new ones. When James Joyce was asked if the words in the dictionary were not numerous enough for him, he said, yes, but they are not the right ones.

FICTION AND ACTUALITY

The important distinction for students of literature between what is *true* and what is *real* can be illustrated by the newspaper item which tells us that Mr. Z, a recluse for fifty years who appeared to his neighbors as a professional ragpicker, died last week and, to everyone's astonishment, left in his mattress $75,000 in one-dollar bills and thirty-five shares of AT&T. The story of Mr. Z is real in that it actually happened according to publicly verifiable evidence. But it lacks the quality of truth because, although we know that such things can and do happen, we also suspect that they are not likely and, moreover, that they do not, despite their being possible, convincingly present the nature of our society or the way things, in essence, are. Poverty is not, as a rule, an eccentric disguise for wealth.

The writer of fiction does not abandon interesting material, however; he confronts it. If the story of Mr. Z is real but untrue, it is the writer's function to find, if not *the* truth about American life, at least *a* truth about American life by re-presenting the story of Mr. Z in such a way as to make his improbable career seem likely. He will do this by employing the devices of style: exposition, characterization, tone, pace, proportion, mood, setting, design, and — the burden of this chapter — narrative point of view.

The writer can also write well or badly. That is to say, there are, as Remy De Gourmont put it, "writers who write and writers who don't write," by which he meant that there are writers who care about style and writers who do not. By style, as we have said, he did not mean idiosyncrasy or mannerism. He meant the way in which the written work is carefully and consciously put together.

There have been writers like Theodore Drieser who felt that what they had to say, however they said it, was enough; and now there is the contemporary writer who feels that what there is to say, however it is said, is too much to deal with. De Gourmont did not say that the subject matter of a work of fiction is irrelevant to its worth. He did say, however, that "the books of the past which still live, live only by virtue of their style," and that, quoting Buffon, "all the relations which constitute style, are so many truths quite as useful for the mind as those forming the subject. . . ."

Mr. Roth, plainly, is a writer who *does* write. He knows well enough that all fiction, whether tied to actual happenings or not, is artificial; that whether it is about Benny Bedwell or Beowulf, it is all about men, women, and children and not much else; and that the life it imitates is somewhat unbelievable and without *any* guaranteed reality of its own until the writer transforms it and shapes it into a *different* world and then, by the strength of his rhetoric, induces us to come *into* this world and accept it as true.

On the same day that the Grimes girls were being murdered, the Chicago Cubs might have lost their tenth in a row. In the light of eternity, what could be less important? A novelist who did not think so would be trifling. Baseball is only a game; the Grimes girls were flesh and blood. To date no one has claimed to have made a novel out of the Grimes case, but some-one doubtless will. Meanwhile one of the finest novels in years, Bernard Malamud's *The Natural,* a book about a ballplayer, deals with various aspects of an American myth with an admir-able combination of low humor and high seriousness. There-fore, when the contemporary American novelist says he can scarcely make fiction out of the facts of American life, one is moved to ask, "Which facts?" The big ones, the small ones, the green ones, the blue ones? The writer *does* have his pick. The factual subject matter of fiction has to be evaluated, true enough, if literature is to be more than mere esthetic exercise. But who will say that a story about the bombing of Hiroshima is necessarily more important than one about going down the Mississippi in a raft, especially when one considers that they are both about the same thing, human responsibility, except that the one about the raft is perhaps better written. Mark Schorer does not overstate the case when he says, "technique alone objectifies the materials of art; hence technique alone eval-uates those materials. . . . And the final lesson about the mod-ern novel is that . . . technique not only contains intellectual and moral implications, but it discovers them."

Now, let's look at Mr. Roth's technique. When he refers to his account of the Grimes case as "a story," he does so prop-erly, for intentionally or not, he has made literature out of life, fiction out of fact. He has done this by making use of certain devices characteristic of narrative fiction.

THE AUTHOR THE READER KNOWS

First of all Mr. Roth has added another character to the cast, perhaps the most decisive character of all—himself; more-over, this character is endowed with an *invented* personality, a persona, or mask, if you will. He is Roth-the-immediate-story-teller, as distinguished from Roth-the-author-of-books. One exists as a voice in his work; the other, say, owns a home in Bucks County. The author who exists as a voice in his work, whose reality the reader must imagine, is the implied or em-pirical author. He is the author the reader must know, for he is the one who tells the reader what to think.

The implied author, in this case, who writes, "Several winters back, while I was living in Chicago, the city was shocked and mystified. . . ." is, moreover, a voice no less fictional because it is heard in an expository essay than is, say, the voice heard at the outset of a novel, the fictional voice that says to us, "Call me Ishmael," or the voice which advises us that, "Happy families are all alike," or the one which allows that, "One might as well begin with Helen's letters to her sister." When Frank O'Connor begins a story with: "Even if there were only two men left in the world and both of them saints, they wouldn't be happy," he is taking pains to establish in the mind of the reader an *image* of an author who may be, in point of fact, very unlike the *real* living author, and to that degree—to the degree that he is idealized—he is a fictional character. At the same time that he must get on with his story, the writer must establish some sort of workable relationship with the reader. In the O'Connor instance, it is one of trust. The reader here will take the author for a person of urbane wit and folk wisdom.

In discussing this aspect of the rhetoric of fiction, Wayne Booth cites Holden Caulfield's remark at the beginning of *The Catcher in the Rye:* "What really knocks me out," Holden says, "is a book that, when you're all done reading it, you wish the author that wrote it was a terrific friend of yours and you could call him up on the phone whenever you felt like it." If Mr. Roth as implied author does not want you to feel that you can call him up any time you feel like it, he does want you to feel that if you met him at a party, and he decided to talk to you, you ought to be quiet and listen. It should be understood that we are not talking about the man who wrote the article, the real author, the Mr. Roth whom we have never met; we are referring to the fictional narrator whom the author has invented, and whom he has clothed in a public personality in order to induce us to accept the norms of *his* world as valid ones.

THE READER THE AUTHOR INVENTS

One might point out, in this connection, that the magazines *Commentary* and *Partisan Review* and others of that sort are likely never to become popular because more often than not the public voices of their writers provide the average reader with a distasteful *fictional* image of the implied authors to whom these voices belong. Privately, these authors may be paragons of respectability and, in their style of life, mild-mannered champions of the status quo; publicly, however, in their *prose* style as distinguished from their *life* style, they are more or less suspect, more or less subversive, more or less irreverent. This style is a mask easy to put on because it is often provided by the tone of the publication itself. The magazine often has available a built-in stance and an *implied readership* as well as an implied authorship. The first editors of *The New Yorker* magazine announced that their publication would not be for "the old lady from Dubuque," thus, presumably, assuring the magazine a qualitative success, at least. For her part, the old lady still finds *The New Yorker* incredible. And that's the way *The New Yorker* wants it. On the other hand, the critic Edmund Wilson said recently that whenever he chances to look at *Life* magazine he gets the odd feeling that he does not live in this country.

Mr. Roth, then, might as well have *intended* to write *narrative fiction* in his account of the Grimes case, because he has invented a character to tell his tale, he has established a distinct and meaningful tone, and he has, moreover, even invented an audience that will accept it. He has reason to believe that his implied reader will accept as congenial the tone of voice of his implied author and enter willingly into *his* world as if it were real and true.

One supposes, therefore, that it would be *less* important to know for a fact that there was or was not a man named Homer, that he did or did not write the *Iliad* first—that it would be less important to establish these facts than it would be to identify the empirical Homer, to hear accurately the sound of his narrative voice, so that one might know how the author behind the voice wants the reader to evaluate the world of Heroic Greece, even when there is no one at hand to tell him. If the public virtues are celebrated in the *Iliad* and the domestic virtues are celebrated in the *Odyssey*, perhaps the reader should listen hard for that muted fictional voice which says here: I mean *this*; and there: I only *half* mean this; and in still another place: I don't really mean this at all; but in any case, you can *trust* me because, like God, I, Homer, am probably an old man with a gray beard.

DISTANCE AS A FACT OF STYLE

Northrop Frye has reminded us that the expression *esthetic distance* is redundant, because "esthetic" *means* distance. There is no literary art, no imaginative writing without the author's standing back, disassociating himself, somehow, from his material. Jonathan Swift had to invent Gulliver to tell his story. Gulliver is both interesting and amusing in his deadpan accounts of amazing voyages, but Swift himself, for all his wit and sophistication, might have been too pointed and overbearing as the narrator of *Gulliver's Travels*. Moreover, there is only so much unstyled, unfictionalized reality that any reader can take, even those who are willing to look hard at the human condition.

Finally, the nature and degree of distance helps define the writer's meaning. Mr. Roth's essay, having cited the Grimes case as the *real* America, establishes a narrative tone, or voice, which has the effect of keeping his grisly material at arm's length and makes it possible for the reader to take it in without becoming sickened. Roth avoids equally the wail of the romantic and the self-righteousness of the social crusader. He does not bespatter the page with the poet's own blood, and he does not make any miraculous claims for the secret ballot. What does he do? He hazards, in effect, a definition of contemporary American life, the life he claims to be practically impossible for the imaginative author to define. He defines it as much by his method as by his matter. He defines it as comedy and his tone is satiric. The Grimes girls were flesh and blood, but they do not bleed in Roth's prose.

Roth's method, then, bears some resemblance to that of another social satirist of another country and another time, Voltaire. Erich Auerbach describes Voltaire's method as the "searchlight technique," which "*overilluminates* the ridiculous, the absurd or the repulsive." He speaks of Voltaire's ". . . tempo, his rapid, keen summary of development, his quick shifting of scenes, his surprisingly sudden confronting of things which are not usually seen together . . . dreadful incidents appear comic because they come hammering down with slapstick speed." Take for example the following passage from *Candide:*

"I was in my bed in a deep sleep, when it pleased
heaven to send the Bulgarians into our fair castle . . . ;
they cut my father's throat and my brother's and chopped
my mother to pieces. A huge Bulgarian, six feet tall, observing that I had fainted at the sight, began to rape me;
that brought me to, I recovered consciousness, I screamed,
I struggled, I bit, I scratched, I tried to tear out the Bulgarian's eyes, not knowing that everything that was happening in my father's castle was perfectly customary; the
brute gave me a knife thrust in my left side, of which I
still bear the scar." "Alas, I hope that I shall see it,"
said the simple Candide. "You shall see it," said Cunegonde; "but let us go on." "Go on," said Candide.

We have Cunegonde's word for it that what "was happening
. . . was perfectly customary," as we have Roth's word for it
that in Chicago "one week's dismemberment fades into
the next's." The maiden's brutal account of her experience at
the hands of the Bulgarian rapist turns, as Auerbach points out,
into a kind of erotic quip, analogous to the teachers of the
Grimes girls reporting that "they had no hobbies."

In the first three sentences Mr. Roth does much to establish the quality of the narrator's voice and through it that distance from his subject matter essential to his satirical method:

Several winters back, while I was living in Chicago, the
city was shocked and mystified by the death of two teen-age
girls. So far as I know the populace is mystified still; as for
the shock, Chicago is Chicago, and one week's dismemberment
fades into the next's. The victims this particular year were
sisters.

One hears in these words the voice of the ironist, the voice
of a speaker who pretends. He pretends to be what he is not,
and he pretends to mean *only* what he says. With the sardonic
"one week's dismemberment fades into the next's," he pretends
to be only characterizing the city's basic indifference behind its
feigned shock and mystification. Moreover, he pretends to be
too hardened and too world-weary to protest against the horror.

But he *is* protesting, although he does not say, "Oh, isn't all this dehumanization horrible!" This the reader already knows and understandably does not want to be reminded of. What the reader wants is to know how to respond to the horror so that he can tolerate his own feelings by intellectualizing them, rendering them object rather than subject. The implication is, further, that Chicagoans are more curious than conscientious about murder. Who, then, really cares about the humanity involved? The author cares, despite his mask of detachment, and the reader cares because the author has induced him to do so. The humorous tone is a way of saying that the death of the two girls by itself is no laughing matter, but that if one gets far enough back from it, as the writer makes us do, one must see it as part of a larger human action which *is* funny. It is funny in the way in which it dramatizes the human condition as some kind of self-delusion.

The author's mask of detachment, his pretended inability to recall details ("One paper, I forget which" and "A strange man steps forward, by the name of Shultz or Schwartz—I don't really remember") is an offhandedness which is more apparent than real, and which does more than simply argue that the Grimes case is a bad dream. Furthermore, this offhandedness is belied by the author's careful attention to other details elsewhere in the narrative—the kinds of details the writer of fiction finds indispensable for establishing character and setting: the movie, an Elvis Presley; the car, a Cadillac, not a Chevrolet; a pink Cadillac, not a black one; the suit, a one-button roll. The fragments of dialogue are carefully selected to define both the speaker and the parties to the case: "yeah, she was all right, yeah, she was popular"; "I never thought any boy of mine would do a thing like that"; and finally, "Imagine me in that kitchen!"

Benny Bedwell and the Grimes girls are probably no easier to invent than Charles Van Doren, but to the storyteller, the maker of fiction, they are there to be used for whatever their short, wretched lives might have meant. It is not lost on the author that Benny decides he will become a carpenter, that unmistakably Christian occupation. In the end (and you will notice that it is *precisely* at the end) the author speaks of the parakeets. After that what is there to say? Mr. Roth is quick to seize on the ready-made symbol. Not only are the Grimes girls dead, but their very memories are dehumanized in the form of two of nature's most idiotic creatures. One need not go into the possibilities of the names "Babs" and "Pattie" and of "Benny Bedwell" for a seducer of young movie fans, except to say that in choosing first to include, and then to emphasize, these details in his narrative, the writer has exercised an artistic choice.

It is the argument of the contemporary fiction writer that this age satirizes *itself*, thereby leaving the artist without technical means. This is apparently not quite so. It was Mr. Roth, who with freedom of artistic choice, selected the Grimes case to write about in the first place, and it was his storyteller's sure instinct that told him not to try to elicit crocodile tears over the mothers of the unfortunate youngsters who only craved a chance to act out a real, live soap opera.

It would seem then that rather than satirizing itself, American life tends to melodrama, which we understand to be comedy without humor. If there is to be true satire, if there is to be that blend of criticism and wit by which human frailty is held up to ridicule, the writer of narrative fiction can and does provide it today, even as he did a hundred years ago. Huck Finn's experiences in various river communities are both frightening and hilarious, as are Tod Hacket's experiences with the grotesques of Hollywood in Nathanael West's *The Day of the Locust*. If it is *not* a tribute to his readers, it is, perhaps, to Twain himself, that his great novel is still taken to be a book for children. In any case, whether it is Huck witnessing a near lynching or Odysseus' men watching their leader play fast and loose with their lives in order to tease a one-eyed monster, the subject matter tells the writer how he shall tell his story; and, conversely, style, *how he tells his story*, gives meaning to the subject matter.

Whatever the disagreements over Shakespeare's plays in the learned numbers of the *Shakespeare Quarterly,* in the pages of *Show Biz,* that frantic chronicle of the amusement industry, *Julius Caesar* and *Romeo and Juliet* are characterized respectively as "boffola b. o." and a "$330,000 setback."[1] It is not for nothing that the drama is depicted with two heads. The smiling and frowning masks are those of Comedy and Tragedy, but perhaps they are also the smile of the Biz as it jollies audiences and placates leading ladies, and the anguish of Literature at such goings-on. In thinking about drama one must remember that it is of the stage, not the page, and that once on the page it struggles toward the footlights.

DRAMA AND SHOW BUSINESS

Drama differs from other types of literature not only as they differ from one another—in form—but also in being designed for collaborative performance before a collective audience. When Horatio tries to convince Hamlet that the Ghost is indeed the ghost of the former king of Denmark, he says:

These hands are not more like.

We admire here the specifically dramatic invention which evokes the gestural art of the actor in the writing. The alternation of

1 Abel Green and Joe Laurie, Jr., *Show Biz* (Garden City, New York: Doubleday, 1952), pp. 404, 524.

scenes in *Hamlet* from the open platform (where Hamlet first encounters the Ghost, to the more "private" playing areas (the
"closet"where he reproaches his mother, the room where the King
kneels unable to pray) is not only an effort at variety, it is the
writer's exploitation of the physical resources of the stage to characterize the forces opposed in the play. The poet and the fiction
writer use one language, or possibly two, if we include the typo-
graphical effects some of them employ to convey meaning. The
dramatist, however, uses not only a verbal language but a language of objects (stage properties and costumes), of volume (set
design), of nonverbal sounds (music and "effects"), of gesture
and motion (the actor's "business" and the dancer's choreog-
raphy), and of light and color. All these languages he strives
to control, as Shakespeare tried to control gesture in the line
just quoted. But the dramatist cannot control them fully. Even
the director cannot. The dramatist cannot, in fact, control even
what the actor finally speaks. In Hamlet's instructions to the
players who visit his castle at Elsinore, instructions that they
keep to the script, there is surely something of Shakespeare's annoyance at Elizabethan actors who substituted their own inven-
tions for his lines. The plays we read, then, are only one aspect
—though the most important one—of the dramatic performance. And the performance, not the printed play, is the dramatist's ultimate concern, despite his limited control of it.

   Further, both play and performance are intended for a collective audience, and we must take this into account in considering the dramatist's art. For one thing, the audience in part
determines the length of the play. A poet may write a two-line
epigram, a novelist a sprawling chronicle in many volumes. But
the dramatist must consider the evening's dinner and the night's
sleep, and how large a mass he moves in assembling an audience for the time between. One does not gather several hundred
people to hear an epigram, and even the wittiest nine-act play
is no match in appeal for the last commuter train. The dramatist must stay close to the Shakespearian "two hours' traffic of
the stage." In other ways, too, the fact of the collective audience
determines what and how the dramatist writes. He must sacrifice subtleties of detail in language to the need that his audience
understand the play on first hearing—unless, like Shakespeare,
he knows how to be subtle and direct at once. And he cannot
draw for two hours on the intensity of feeling and concentration

that the lyric poet maintains for perhaps fifty lines. Nor is the dramatist's work long enough or of such a nature as to absorb successfully the stretches of exposition that the reader of a novel will tolerate—such matter as the digressions on whales and whaling in *Moby Dick*.

Such considerations of audience and performance do not figure so importantly in analyses of lyric and fiction. For this reason, the drama is possibly the most difficult of literary forms to analyze. In considering lyric and narrative we are concerned primarily with the meaning and relations of one part of the work to another. But in considering why a scene in a play is written as it is, we must ask not only how the scene relates to other scenes, but quite frequently how it was shaped by "external" considerations relating to production and performance. At any rate, the drama includes—in the plays of Shakespeare—the most complex problems the student will regularly deal with.

DRAMA AND LYRIC

Our primary concern is understanding drama as a verbal art. From the other kinds of verbal art—lyric and narrative— it differs radically. Lyric implies a solitary singer, narrative someone who narrates. The drama alone is expressed entirely through many voices. It has technically no *point of view* or *persona* —that is, no invented person through whom the work is transmitted.

In some works these ancient and essential distinctions between drama and the other verbal arts seem blurred. In lyric verse, for example, persons other than the imagined *I* are referred to and even speak. In Shelley's over quoted sonnet "Ozymandias," for example, the first lines

> I met a traveller from an antique land
> Who said:

are followed, for the rest of the poem, by the traveller's description of the time-shattered monument to the tyrant Ozymandias. But the traveller does not speak in his own right—that is, he has no psychological identity, no role in the poem distinct from the identity and role of the *I* who quotes him. He is only a vehicle for the libertarian opinions and the satisfied awe of the *I*.

The question to be asked about "Ozymandias" is not whether it is dramatic, but what self-consciousness or uncertainty caused Shelley to make an unreal division in the persona (invented speaker) of the poem.

Contrast this instance with what occurs typically in drama. Characters in a play—unlike the quasi-character of the persona in "Ozymandias"—do not allow one another to speak because they agree with one another or think one another important. They speak because the action and significance of the play cannot be communicated through or by one person. Essentially the lyric is a cry, an intense concentration of attitude and feeling. To achieve such an effect more than one character is too many. Thus the characters mentioned or even speaking directly in a lyric become—as did the traveller in "Ozymandias"—merely the occasions for the persona's feelings and predications.

We can understand something more of the difference between lyric and drama by observing what happens when lyric forms are employed in the body of a play. Classic instances are to be found in Shakespeare's *Romeo and Juliet*. The two lovers declare their mutual attraction in a sonnet in Act I, scene 5, lines 95–108. The meter and rhyme scheme here are those of the conventional Shakespearean sonnet, but in the theatre the lines are almost unrecognizable as a sonnet. We do not hear them as an entity apart from the rest of the scene; they are assimilated into its action. That we recognize the sonnet form upon a close reading does not add to our understanding of the characters or of the action of the play but only to our impression of Shakespeare's technical virtuosity. Yet this is a distraction from the play and, further, may convince us that perhaps Shakespeare himself was somehow distracted from his task, doodling elegantly as he expended care that does not affect the way we view the first encounter of the lovers.

When lyric passages are effective in drama, as they are in the many songs scattered through Shakespeare's plays, they become moments of special intensity whose meaning depends on the context of character or event, or they act as ornamented changes in texture which, again, require the context of surrounding material before they can be appreciated. Their expressiveness as isolated lyric poetry is much less than their expressiveness as part of the play. They act as does any other speech in

drama, not as a self-contained unit of meaning and emotion—
that is, as lyric—but as utterance largely dependent for its sense
and feeling on the utterance of others.

Yet lyric and drama do join in what is called the *dramatic
monologue,* or the *dramatic lyric,* of which Browning's "My Last
Duchess" and some of the shorter poems of Donne are good
examples. It is worth considering the form because it illustrates
through exception the commonplace that the imprint of individual "character" is often weaker on lyric, which employs a
single persona, than on drama, which employs many characters. Some of the reasons for this are obvious. We observe qualities through observing contrasts, and the lyric does not typically offer us contrasts of alternative personae. Moreover, the
aspects of character are more various in drama because of the
variety of plot contexts in which character may be exhibited;
and often these aspects of the persona in a lyric are restricted
or swallowed up by its intense unity of feeling and predication.
Finally, the language of lyric—to use Coleridge's phrase—"calls
attention to itself." It is not, of course, a wholly opaque medium
through which we see nothing at all of the persona. But our
attention is so often directed to, and so much remains with, the
subtleties and achievements of the language in lyric, that we
assign the capacity to attain such richness of language as a dominant share of the character of the lyric voice. The lyric persona
is, typically, a singer first and only afterward a lover, a revolutionary, a conqueror, or a victim. On the other hand, the language of drama (and one need mention as example here only
the name of Shakespeare) is not wholly transparent. It can en-
gross an almost endless attention. But typically and at its best,
dramatic language is the "distillation of personality." The characters of Shakespeare's plays are first kings or fools, fathers or
sons, and the adroitness of their language is something that does
not define them as poets. Rather it defines the heightened ten-
sions of the dramatic situations they move in. Moreover, the
language of drama also serves the plot. We attempt to peer
through dramatic language at the shadows of events to come
and how we are to perceive them. This role of language as a cue
to coming events is rarely important in lyric. The "outcome"
of the "Ozymandias" sonnet is known to us as soon as we have
read the words "vast and trunkless legs of stone."

Our interest in lyric, then, is so much in the language itself that when we see beyond language to a highly individualized character we are surprised into giving the work the distinguishing name of *dramatic monologue,* or *dramatic lyric.* The special role of language in drama, its extensive though not exclusive referability to character and action, is what Macaulay had in mind when he wrote that the fault of tragedy was eloquence, and the fault of comedy wit. Both eloquence and wit may call too much attention to themselves to be truly "dramatic."

DRAMA AND NARRATIVE

If we contrast narrative with drama, we see even more clearly the close relation between character and the language of drama. There is a passage in Holinshed's *Chronicle* that deals with a parliament held in the reign of Henry V, and specifically with a bill "exhibited" during the previous reign and now revived for discussion.

> The effect of which supplication [so reads Holinshed] was, that the temporall lands devoutlie giuen, and disordinatlie spent by religious, and other spirituall persons, should be seized into the kings hands, sith the same might suffice to mainteine, to the honor of the king, and defense of the realme, fifteene earles, fifteene hundred knights, six thousand and two hundred esquiers, and a hundred almesse-houses, for reliefe onelie of the poore, impotent, and needie persons, and the king to have cleerlie to his coffers twentie thousand pounds, with manie other provisions and values of religious houses, which I passe over.
>
> This bill was much noted, and more feared among the religious sort, whom suerlie it touched verie neere. . . .[2]

Holinshed's point of view is largely that of an objective narrator. The contrast between the words *devoutlie giuen* and *disordinatlie spent* is observation; its moral implications belong to the bill and to the forces in Commons who introduced it. The

2   Raphael Holinshed, *The Third Volume of Chronicles* (1587 edition). The text of this passage is easily available in *Narrative and Dramatic Sources of Shakespeare,* ed. Geoffrey Bullough (New York: Columbia University Press, 1962), IV, 377.

references to knights, earls, and almshouses are statistical, defining the amount of money involved. The passage puts before us a struggle between the Church and Commons over the sources of taxation.

Shakespeare transforms this narrative passage into the speeches opening *Henry V*. The Archbishop of Canterbury's conversation with the Bishop of Ely follows Holinshed almost to the letter.

Canterbury speaks:

> It must be thought on. If it pass against us,
> We lose the better half of our possesion;
> For all the temporal lands which men devout
> By testament have given to the Church
> Would they strip from us; being valued thus:
> As much as would maintain, to the king's honour,
> Full fifteen earls and fifteen hundred knights,
> Six thousand and two hundred good esquires;
> And, to relief of lazars and weak age,
> Of indigent faint souls past corporal toil,
> A hundred almshouses right well supplied;
> And to the coffers of the king beside,
> A thousand pounds by the year. Thus runs the bill.

Ely replies: "This would drink deep," and Canterbury: "'Twould drink the cup and all."

By moving the words from a narrative to a dramatic frame, Shakespeare completely alters their meaning and effect. Before, the words were a largely objective statement of a political struggle. Now they have become the Archbishop of Canterbury's rather sinister self-exposure. The references to knights and almshouses, before merely statistical, now are evidence of the worldliness and cynicism of an Archbishop who too readily equates the relief of lepers with the maintenance of Earls, and whose speech implies that he makes no ethical distinctions between the two. The phrase "which men devout have given to the Church" becomes ironic. What emerges from the speech is not so much the struggle over taxation as the character of the Archbishop. The dramatic frame both establishes and alters the meaning of the language, and this dramatic frame is in the first place the frame of character.

We expect of the storyteller that he will spin his tale of men's changing fortunes. We expect of the lyric poet that he will create a fancy in which feelings and predications are wondrous, plausible, and complete. And of the dramatist we expect that he will wring character from language. Yet it is not so simple. Persons in a play may seem characterless, whether through the playwright's inability or through design, and the teller of the tale and the imagined voice of a poem are also characters. But in the reading of a story we observe first its action; in the reading of lyric, its verbal fancy; and in the consideration of a drama we first observe character, from which the language of drama comes as from a mold.

The special quality of language in drama, then, derives from the dramatic context which assigns language to living actors. This context transforms language, whether or not the dramatist is skilled in promoting the transformation, into the distinctive and immediate expression of a character at a given moment. It is useful to think of dramatic language as gesture, as much a part of the actor's expression as a movement of his hand. Taken selectively, verbal gestures make up individual characters in a drama. Taken in sum, they make up its action. This manner of presentation, and, therefore, the way in which we experience drama—this going from verbal gesture to individual character, from individual character to action—is what makes for the immediacy of drama as a form, for what we call loosely, but not wholly without justice, its "reality." What we face in our unordered experience of life is not all things composed as if by single voice, or point of view, as in lyric or narrative, but each thing in its separate voice. In this sense even props and scenery are speakers. Though drama is no more unordered experience than are the other arts, it alone confronts us with something nearly like unordered experience's manyness of voices.

In the technical sense, then, drama has no unifying point of view. This has important implications. Between us and the events of a lyric or a tale stands a singer or a teller. If he is active, explaining, he casts these events into some explanatory sequence. If he is passive, he nonetheless seems to limit the events to what may be known or felt by a single person. Drama, then, must always appear a literary form less reducible than the others to simple propositions or feelings, for drama is not only presented through many men; it is what no single man can tell. In *Moby Dick,* Ishmael survives to relate the struggle of Ahab with the great whale. This suggests that Melville's titanic fable may be contained, in some sense comprehended, by the attitudes of an Ishmael.[3] But when Hamlet, dying, says to Horatio:

> Absent thee from felicity awhile,
> And in this harsh world draw thy breath in pain,
> To tell my story

we know that Horatio cannot do it. He can be no Ishmael. For even his flexible intelligence has foundered on the multiple meanings of the play. He, like all other characters in the drama, is finite, another voice which does not speak the whole of things.

CHARACTER IN DRAMA

For this reason the actor, referring to the character he must play, calls it—with perhaps unconscious accuracy—a *part.* But it is a part reducible to other parts. We do not ordinarily perceive ourselves as "constructed": our self-consciousness conceives an infinitely complex web of elements it cannot readily disentangle. But fortunately character in literature, and dramatic character specifically, is less complex and less intricately organized than human character. Its three major elements can usefully be called *identity, will,* and *role.*

We may define *identity* as a set of ethically neutral physical or psychic traits: height, for example, or a gigantic nose, or a dislike of bread, or the complex fact of being a Venetian. *Will,* on the other hand, is not ethically neutral. It is the exercise of ethically important options. How it may appear in even a brief passage is well illustrated by an exchange between Hamlet and his schoolmate Rosencrantz, who has been sent by King Claudius to spy on the prince. Rosencrantz is asked why he just then

3 On this point see Murray Krieger, *The Tragic Vision* (New York: Holt, Rinehart and Winston, 1960), pp. 249 ff.

laughed at Hamlet's statement: "Man delights me not." The reply is revealing. Rosencrantz laughed at the thought of the poor reception that the touring actors would get at the castle as a result of Hamlet's misanthropy. Hamlet immediately responds that he intends to make the actors welcome indeed. The contrast here—a contrast of *will*—is between Rosencrantz' callousness and Hamlet's charity.

Hamlet's apparent misanthropy ("Man delights me not"), though it, too, seems to imply *will*, is related to Hamlet's *role*. After his father's ghost has cried out to him for revenge on Claudius, Hamlet has taken on, though not without serious reserva- tions, the role of Avenger, and his melancholy bitterness is one of the traits associated with that role. *Role* is perhaps best under- stood as a highly conventionalized course of behavior. The roles that figure importantly in actual experience are not necessarily important in drama. For example, professional and occupa- tional roles (doctor, lawyer, businessman) are submerged in dramatic roles, which derive primarily from the major inter- personal relations (son, lover, husband, father), for drama is not concerned with the world's work but with the world's pas- sions. Even roles associated with public life (king, prince, presi- dent) are subtly merged or made parallel with these inter- personal roles. We recognize the process when we speak of George Washington as "the father of his country." Thus King Lear, in abdicating and dividing his kingdom and disinheriting his one faithful daughter, treats his subjects as he treats his child. His irresponsible political behavior is an aspect of his parental errors.

Further, dramatic roles are limited in number not only through this convergence on the interpersonal—which arouses and engages the strongest feelings—but also through the theat- rical conventions (accepted practices) of an era or a dramatic type (comedy, for example). Each period of drama and kind of drama has a distinctive gallery of stock roles on which the dram- atist may draw. The "New" Comedy of Greece, best repre- sented by the works of Menander, had its young-heiress-in- disguise, its young-man-kept-in-check-by-his-father, its *senex* or old-man-who-interferes-with-the-lovers, its witty-servant-who- brings-the-lovers-together. These stock roles persist in later comedy, though modified by fashion and individual talent. To understand a play fully, one must have a knowledge of the current stock roles. Such knowledge is almost indispensable lest one confuse the common attributes of a role with the particularities of identity or will. In reading *Hamlet,* for example, one must know something of the role of the Avenger, a common and important one in Elizabethan tragedy. A lack of this knowledge can lead to a confusion between individual identity or will and conventional role in one's reading of Hamlet's speeches. This sort of confusion is sprinkled through the interminable commentary on Hamlet's character, commentary in which the traits an Elizabethan audience would associate only with the role of Avenger form the basis of mistaken speculations about Hamlet's psychic identity.

The distinct yet related components of identity, will, and role may be further clarified by example. To be stout is a trait of *identity,* ethically neutral, merely descriptive. But when an enormous girth is spoken of as King Henry speaks of Falstaff's paunch in the stern injunction: "Leave off gourmandizing," it becomes an instance of *will,* here the exercise of a bad ethical option. The sin of gluttony, however, is associated with the role of the Vice or Lord of Misrule, the traditional figure who presides—as does Falstaff in Shakespeare's Henry plays—over the license of Carnival until he is banished by reason and order. The jolly fat man as Lord of Misrule (unwonted jollity) has many variants; perhaps the persistence of the role is best, if surprisingly, illustrated in the ample figure of Santa Claus, who was —interestingly enough—also the patron saint of thieves.

The sometimes fine distinctions between *identity, role,* and *will* as components of dramatic character must be emphasized because of our tendency, mentioned earlier, to think of human character as indivisible, and because of the strengthening of this tendency by the vividness of the actor's performance. But in actuality the dramatist may exercise many options in his creation of character, omitting one element, emphasizing another, or permitting the elements to interact or to remain separate from one another. The options that the dramatist exercises determine the nature of a character and its appropriateness to one or another kind of play. What follows is a necessarily incomplete consideration of the major options.

Generally, the more important a character in a play, the

more likely it is that he will be made up of all three elements. A minor character—what the actor would call a "walk-on"— is usually no more than a role, as are the servants who bring in dinner in *Macbeth*. If the characters have sufficiently important roles, they may be given scraps of identity or will. Thus the murderers in *Macbeth*, though they appear quite briefly, are shown to be of savage and bitter dispositions. But they are allowed only so much *will* as suits them for their roles. They have no identities whatever; they are, in fact, called only First and Second Murderer, and Shakespeare may not have bothered even to count the number he created.

Identity   Sometimes the author may suppress identity to emphasize the kind of will or ethical option that the suppression implies: Shakespeare does this twice in creating the "yes-men" King Claudius employs in *Hamlet*. Both Cornelius and Voltimand seem to forfeit their identities when they answer the King in unison:

> In that, and all things, will we show our duty.

Rosencrantz and Guildenstern, also willing tools, are treated as without identity when the King says:

> Thanks, Rosencrantz and gentle Guildenstern.

and the Queen adds:

> Thanks, Guildenstern and gentle Rosencrantz.

Thus the dramatist calls our attention to his creation of barely human ciphers who take on roles that require a tainted will. This implication is appropriately stronger in the case of Rosencrantz and Guildenstern, who spy on their friend Hamlet, than in the case of Cornelius and Voltimand, who serve in more proper business.

However, characters of major importance may also be created with very little attention to identity. Characters in symbolic dramas or in the *morality plays* of the middle ages are often without ethically neutral distinguishing traits. Allegorical per-

sonages like Everyman or Discord have quite generalized physical or psychic traits, or where they have distinctive traits these
are related to some aspect of their role. At the other extreme,
realistic or naturalistic drama employs characters we are asked
to accept as lifelike (to be encountered in everyday social traffic) by virtue of their many tangible identifying marks. It should
be apparent, however, that when specific traits of identity,
whether physical or psychological, are present in great number,
the character differs more from our notions of common humanity
than does a figure in allegory. Such is the case in modern psychological drama, where motivations are made so extensive and
specific that we are presented with figures who become objects
of study because of their distinctiveness and eccentricity rather
than objects of compassion because of their common humanity.

Yet ethically neutral traits, sparingly employed, may serve
to unite characters with common humanity as well as to separate them from it. Some of the most moving scenes in drama
occur when common features of identity are suddenly revealed
beneath a distastefully presented role or a tainted will. Thus
Shylock, in a famous speech in the third act of *The Merchant of
Venice,* cries out:

> I am a Jew. Hath not a Jew eyes? hath not a Jew hands,
> organs, dimensions, senses, affections, passions? fed with
> the same food, hurt with the same weapons, subject to the
> same diseases, healed by the same means, warmed and
> cooled by the same winter and summer as a Christian is?

Will   The obscuring or even total elimination of *will* as
an element in character is quite common in comedy and in recent serious drama, but it is apparently inappropriate for the
central figures in the greatest serious dramas. So one concludes
from examining plays that have survived changes in taste.

When the dramatist eliminates will, he may create a character appropriate for a play that embodies the idea of deter-
minism: the idea that men do not, in fact, control their des-
tinies. In recent times such plays have been the product of our
interest in psychological and social forces and our increasing
disbelief in the reality of individual freedom. In the characters
of such plays, role is secondary because, on the determinist

premise, behavior is of little significance; one cataclysmic event —a rape as in a Tennessee Williams play or a mine disaster as in "social" drama—is sufficient to end the almost endless concern with psychological or social identity and thus convince us finally of the paralyzing effects of childhood trauma or social inequity.

But the elimination of will need not be total or consistent or embody a determinist view of men. Comedies abound in characters whose will is in some way obliterated or obscured; the comic ending consists in their regaining it. In farce, for example, will is eliminated or made ineffectual by some mechanical contrivance: one is caught in a revolving door, or one makes love to the wrong twin. The victimized character in farce cannot help doing the "wrong" thing until he gets out of the revolving door or the twins reveal their identities. This last should suggest that in farce identity assumes one of two extremes: it is either ambiguous, so that the twins can render ineffectual the will of another character, or grotesque, as in the case of the character who gets his enormous nose caught in the revolving door and thus cannot exercise his own will.

The dramatist can also limit the will of his characters by psychological means. The result is often a character appropriate for romantic comedy—the lover in the grip of a passion that misdirects or suspends will—as when Titania in *A Midsummer Night's Dream* is blinded to reality and falls in love with an asshead. We speak of such figures as "affected." Thus we distinguish between a misdirection of the will which can be rather easily rectified and—something less easily corrected—an ill will which consistently chooses the bad, or a will working in ignorance. The leading characters in tragedy ordinarily fall into these last two categories. But comedy is kinder; the wills of its major figures are disposed to the good but are obscured or misdirected by passions that temporarily prevent them from acting on what everyone knows. What ends such passionate misdirections of the will in romantic comedy is, sad to say, marriage. The romantic lovers institutionalize their passion and convert it presumably into connubial understanding.

Perhaps the most delightful example of this is the famous "proviso" scene of Congreve's *The Way of the World* in which the lovers Mirabell and Millamant agree on a psychological marriage compact. Millamant's conditions before she will "dwindle to a wife" are precisely the freedom from obsessions that blind the reason and the will of romantic lovers. She wants:

> liberty to pay and receive visits to and from whom I please . . . to wear what I please . . . to have no obligation upon me to converse with wits that I don't like, because they are your acquaintance; or to be intimate with fools because they may be your relations. . . . And lastly, wherever I am, you shall always knock at the door before you come in.

Her conditions overthrow the limitations of romantic passion, and indeed even some of the limitations customary in marriage. But they illustrate perfectly the frame of mind of characters who, at the end of romantic comedies, recover their wills from their roles. If Millamant's insistence on her freedom seems to promise trouble in the future, it is a sign of the link that joins comic and serious, even tragic, characters. For in tragedy the typical central figure exhibits a disharmony between will and role. So, as the romantic lover recovers his will, he approaches the quality of the serious character whose will is at odds with his role. Millamant, at the end of the proviso scene, resembles Nora, the heroine of Ibsen's *A Doll's House,* who takes her freedom by abandoning her role as wife.

A virtual elimination of will distinguishes not only characters in comedy but also characters in melodrama, the lowest form of theatrical art. This negative judgment on melodrama is not merely a prejudice of criticism. Melodrama pretends to give us characters who act ethically. Yet Rudolph Rassendale (damn his moustache!) could not be other than a villain if he tried, and Hairbreadth Harry (golden-haired, golden-hearted) could not help but pay off the mortgage and so save the fair Belinda from a death worse than fate. In melodrama, ethical option is reduced to identity; it becomes a mere reflex. The appeal of melodrama is only to those who have never known, or have grown weary of, human complexity.

Role The elimination or minimizing of role in major characters can occur, as we saw earlier, when individual action seems to lack significance. It is thus appropriate to characters in plays that convey a determinist outlook or concentrate on the minutiae of individual psychology. In such characters, will, which supports and clarifies role, also dwindles, and both role and will are absorbed into identity: the result is a character like Blanche in Tennessee Williams' *A Streetcar Named Desire,* so much a psychic identity, a product of her past, as to be unable to act. The paradox is that recent professedly "roleless" drama seems to be creating a new set of roles, notable among them the psychological-case-who-is-unable-to-act and the sensitive-young-adult-marked-by-childhood-trauma.

A quite different sort of character is typical of earlier plays. As Bernard Beckerman observed of Elizabethan drama and of Shakespeare in particular,

> At the conclusion of these plays we do not understand the motives of these characters one whit better. Motivation is often assumed. . . .[4]

This seems an extreme statement, but it is wholly accurate. In the mainstream of drama, characterization centers on role and is little concerned with specifying the minutiae of physical or psychic identity. The rumble of instinct and trauma are barely audible—even in a play that seems to offer as much introspection as does *Hamlet*—beneath the continual assertions of will and role. This is a clue to how most earlier drama should be read: we must resist the temptation to put Hamlet on the couch for his melancholy and misogyny and railings against cosmetics. These are not "motivation." They are the marks of the role of the Avenger as surely as a black horse is the mark of the role of Rustler on TV. If one is to speak intelligently of dramatic character, one must know something about the gallery of roles on which the dramatist—however imaginative—relies. This is relatively easy with the theatre of one's own day. When a character in a play by John Osborne fidgets over the London *Times*

4   Bernard Beckerman, *Shakespeare at the Globe* (New York: Macmillan, 1962), p. 149. At this point a remark about *motivation* is appropriate. Its uselessness in analyzing earlier drama is one reason to abandon the term *motivation.* More important is that the term prejudices any analysis. Because it implies the existence of a chain of psychological causes antecedent to dramatic behavior, the term *motivation* does not encourage us to distinguish between instinctive and voluntary behavior, and thus forces all discussions of character to proceed on the narrow assumptions of deterministic psychology.

editorial page, we know he is playing the role of the Angry Young Man; we do not look for birth trauma in the printshop. Though the AYM is a descendant of the role which Hamlet plays, conventions change. To distinguish role from identity we need the specific historical information that comes with wide reading of plays and informed works about them. Without such information our judgments of character are likely to be confused. We can, for example, fail to appreciate the distinction between role and identity, which is central to comedy, or between role and will, which is central to tragedy.

Comedy exploits the amusing possibilities of a disharmony between role and identity. The very titles of some of Molière's plays suggest how the French master of comic drama works identity against role: *The Bourgeois Gentleman, The Doctor in Spite of Himself,* and, if one will allow the male condescension to pass for a moment, *The Lady Intellectuals (Les Précieuses ridicules).* To illustrate further, old age is an aspect of identity to which the role of lover is inappropriate. To create a ninety-year-old flirt is to create a character ripe for the comic theatre. But such a character may also be made to appear pathetic and perhaps even tragic, depending on how the dramatist manipulates the element of will. If will is obscured due to infatuation, there is the possibility of a comic ending in which the toothless Romeo abandons his role as he gains self-knowledge. If, on the other hand, the will is not simply obscured but is being exercised in a perverted way, one has a figure who embodies a monstrous obsession, a figure fit for serious, though perhaps not tragic, drama.

The central figure in tragedy, however, is likely to be created through a disharmony of role and will. We recognize Hamlet, for example, as a man with whom we can sympathize, as one who prefers the good. The role of Avenger is one not wholly appropriate to his will, though he learns to accept it. Hamlet's desperate lines:

> The time is out of joint. Oh, cursed spite
> That ever I was born to set it right

tell us how uneasy he is in the part he must play. His pitiful sighs during the interview in which he realizes he must abandon

Ophelia convince us what anguish it is for him to sacrifice other roles to take up the role of Avenger, to which considerations of duty lead him. Throughout the play, Shakespeare gives us glimpses of "the glass of fashion and the mold of form"—of a Hamlet quite different from the wild creature who exchanges plot for counterplot against Claudius and who breaks Ophelia's heart. In tragic figures, then, role does not flow naturally, let alone inevitably, from identity or even from will. It is in part imposed by circumstances. But the tragic hero is not merely the victim of circumstances. He must assume the unhappy role because the circumstances are ones which a man of good will cannot ignore. Hamlet not only must, he *prefers to,* right an injustice.

An instructive example of the relation between will and role in tragic character is to be found by considering those dialogues of Plato which deal with the death of Socrates. Socrates is condemned because of his opinions to die by drinking hemlock; such is the judgment of the State. When his companions offer Socrates a way of escape, he gently rebukes them. He chooses his death freely because he is old, because he does not fear physical extinction, but above all because he wishes to remain true to his courageous view of things. Our reaction to these dialogues is quite different from our reaction to tragic drama. If pity involves condescension, we can feel no pity for a man who—despite the harsh consequences of the court judgment—has so completely chosen and mastered his fate. His death is not a tragic cutting-off of life; it is life's crown. No tragic feeling results, for will and role are in complete harmony. Socrates embraces this death because he could invent no better.

The case with Hamlet, or with the other great figures in tragedy, is quite different. Though Hamlet accepts his role as Avenger—perhaps a dutiful son could do no less—were he to choose it as whole-heartedly as Socrates chooses the hemlock, we could not but look upon him as bloody-minded or, at the very least, masochistic. The reason for this lies in the difference between the roles of Socrates and Hamlet. The role of martyr-for-the-truth, Socrates' role, is not ethically ambiguous; it is wholly good. Not so Hamlet's role as Avenger. From the very first, the Ghost who urges Hamlet on to revenge sets up impossible conditions: he points out that murder is even "in the best"

most foul, and though he does not specifically enjoin Hamlet to
commit it, there seems no alternative. Despite this, Hamlet is
not to "taint" his mind. The contradiction of a good will coexist-
ing with a morally ambiguous role, or even a role that seems to
demand positively bad behavior, may not seem logical. But it
is the stuff of tragic character.

Aristotle, a tireless examiner of construction in tragic
drama, pointed a way out of this apparent contradiction between will and role with his much misinterpreted idea of catharsis, or purgation. Aristotle thought that in good tragic drama
the playwright discovered means of purging certain roles of the
moral condemnation that would ordinarily attach to them.[5] If
one kills someone by mistake or without being aware of it—
Aristotle reasoned—the taint attached to the role of murderer
is lessened or even entirely cleansed away. The means of reconciling a good will with an infamous or ambiguous role, then,
would seem to lie in the ignorance of whoever performs the role.
Oedipus is the tragic character who seems closest to Aristotle's
formula. In ignorance he kills his father; in ignorance he mar-
ries his mother. And it is only Oedipus' conscientious and self-
less discharge of his duties as king (his good will) that leads to
the discovery of his past. The evil aspect of role is purged and
presented to us as what Aristotle calls *hamartia,* a mistake.

There is something of this sort of solution in *Hamlet.* Hamlet kills Polonius by accident as he lurks behind a great tapestry,
spying on Hamlet's conversation with his mother. But most
tragic figures are not so neatly dealt with as is Oedipus. They
sin not only in ignorance but in carelessness, and sometimes by
choice. But on balance we see them, as we see the almost totally
criminal Macbeth, as having a will not wholly in harmony with
the roles they play. Sometimes this exercise of good will lies only
in the final recognition and acceptance of their past criminality.
In *King Lear* the bastard brother Edmund, villainous and destructive almost to the moment of his death, impresses us as a somewhat tragic figure through the slight grace of a final effort to
help undo his misdeeds.

In any case, we must distinguish the ignorance appropriate

5   The linguistic and historical argument for this view of catharsis may be
found in Gerald F. Else, *Aristotle's Poetics: The Argument* (Cambridge, Mass.:
Harvard University Press, 1958), pp. 423–427.

to tragic figures from the ignorance exhibited by characters in comedy. In both there is an ignorance of self. But in comic characters it springs from a limitation peculiar to the individual. Most often it is a remediable result of an affectation. Thus a brief passion blinds Titania to Bottom's ass-head, and she dotes upon him. Not so in the case of Oedipus. His ignorance seems almost irremediable, something in the nature of the race. Though we know—as did Oedipus—of the predictions that he would become his father's murderer and his mother's bridegroom, we do not dismiss his fate as the just desert of rashness or stupidity. Rather, we sympathize with his anguished protest that "the god Apollo wove this web to trap me." One of the great themes of tragedy is the theme of the limitations of human foresight and human reason, which cannot imagine the complexity of cause and chance or penetrate easily to the actuality of the self. This is quite different from the great theme of comedy—that passion obscures both foresight and reason, and that passion may be overcome.

A final word on the relations of identity, role, and will concerns the relative parsimony with which the dramatist employs them. Common experience confronts us with the changing relations among identity, will, and role. We see the habit of love transform a face, long illness sicken the will, poverty withhold a role. In actual experience the components of character are in constant mutual transformation. Character in drama is less complex. Often this relative simplicity results from the dramatist's concentration on a short span of time during which physical identity, for example, can change very little. But few plays present us—as does *King Lear*—with a spiritual revolution in which a whole psychic make-up is destroyed through madness and reformed after the assumption of a new role. More often the dramatist preserves a significant counterpoint between the various stages of the acting-out of a role and a will or identity which is relatively unaffected by them. Thus, as Hamlet acts out the role of Avenger, we are at various points reminded of continuing traits which unfit him for the role. His sweetness, his intellectuality, his desire for quite other things than violence and intrigue are poignantly referred to by his beloved Ophelia and even by his enemy, the murderer-uncle King Claudius, who remarks that Hamlet is too trusting (hardly a useful trait in an

Avenger) to examine the sword-tip which Claudius has specially exposed and Laertes has poisoned.

OPPORTUNE REMARKS AND CUES

Not everything a character says, however, is referable to identity, will, or role. Such "leftover" statements comprise *cues* and *opportune remarks*. These two categories are important because unless one is clearly aware of them one may mistake them for details of character.

John Holloway aptly describes what we call *cue* in the following passage:

> Where there is no dramatic chorus, the characters speak continually, not perhaps out of character (though sometimes they do even this), but independent of their character, as a kind of running implicit chorus. Their words clarify the situation to the spectator.[6]

Cues range in importance from the casual information:

> Here comes Lucy-Jo!

to the predictive:

> Murder will out!

to the complex interpretive lines of Edgar in *King Lear:*

> When we our betters see bearing our woes,
> We scarcely think our miseries our foes.
> Who alone suffers suffers most i' the mind,
> Leaving free things and happy shows behind.
> But then the mind much sufferance doth o'erskip,
> When grief hath mates, and bearing fellowship.

Though Edgar continues, explaining how his own sufferings have been made more bearable by his understanding of how

6   John Holloway, *The Story of the Night* (Lincoln: University of Nebraska Press, 1963), p. 24.

Lear has suffered, the passage is obviously directed to the audience. It is an attempt to specify how we ought to view the scene before us; how, indeed, we ought to view the fact that we are a collective audience witnessing a tragedy. Spoken cues such as these are a dramatic artifice; they tell us to anticipate one event or to recall another or to look at an event in a certain way. They are in part a compensation for the drama's lack of point of view. How and how often cues are employed depends on the dramatic conventions of different styles and periods. In Greek tragedy the cues as to what the audience was to look for in events were stated primarily by a chorus. Shakespeare assigns cues (often setting them off from the rest of the play by the use of rhymed couplets or aphoristic language) to individual characters, most often, with characteristic irony, to so-called Fools. Modern drama seeks to avoid cues because they are not "realistic," although such plays as Tennessee Williams' *The Glass Menagerie* employ a narrator whose function is sometimes much like that of the Greek chorus.

At any rate, when we read speeches on the page, we see language directed toward several ends: the creation of an identity, the specification of will or role, and the presentation of cues. Sometimes the same phrase or sentence may perform several functions, as when the excited diction and speech rhythm of a cue are also illustrative of a psychological identity. But our major task in examining character is to avoid the errors of interpretation that come from assigning a particular utterance to the wrong category. In Shakespeare, as we noted, cues often come in the form of proverbial statements. It would be wrong to conclude that the character speaking them is the sort of person who falls into platitudes in a moment of crisis.[7]

There are also dramatic utterances that convey neither character nor cue. They may take the form of lines designed to raise a laugh or a tear or to convey what the dramatist fancies to be his wisdom or learning. Such utterances, which serve neither character nor action, are often blemishes in drama. But they are not all due to mere ineptness.

The dramatist is subject to many pressures, not the least among them the pressures to amuse his audience and display

7 See Holloway, pp. 21 ff.

the special talents of his collaborators—the actors and musicians. Ideally the audience should find its entertainment in a play without those momentary pleasures that neither flow from nor contribute to a pleasure in the whole. And ideally actors and musicians should be content to ply their talents within the framework of art. But ideals are rarely realities. So the dramatist will lapse into opportunist gags or sentiment. Audiences do laugh at the mere mention of the word *Brooklyn,* and—as the American showman George M. Cohan discovered—they applaud if you bring on stage (following no matter what fiasco) a large American flag. The author of an opera libretto may find himself writing nothing but occasions for the leading coloratura or the horn section to display its mastery. More legitimately, an evening in the theatre may be little more than opportune statement, as in that often delightful dramatic form, the revue. But its ephemeral nature and its subservience to individual talent is nowhere better indicated than in the typical revue title *New Faces of 1954.* A drama constructed entirely of opportune remarks, however, may also be serious in intent. Some "experimental" dramas in the so-called Theatre of the Absurd attempt to mirror a meaningless, relationless world through a sequence of random utterances. Perhaps the cosmos *is* only a "blooming, buzzing confusion." But if it is, one is tempted to observe, as did the British novelist and critic Rebecca West on a different occasion,

> A copy of the universe is not what is required of art; one of the damned thing is ample.

PLOTS OF ACTION

As the characters play out their roles, events come into being. Whether the events dominate character in the sense that character is only a capacity to participate in them, or whether the characters dominate events in the sense that events are only an effect of character, or whether both characters and events are dominated by ideas, of which they are only illustrations—these are ancient and sometimes fruitless questions, especially if they are considered without reference to particular works. There are even plays in which ideas, characters, and events are all subordinate to the spectacle, the result being a quality like that of ritual. But it is useful to know that—despite the recent interest in them —psychological and problem or thesis plays (in which events are subordinate to character or ideas) are a minority among the plays that have survived changes in taste.

Yet the dominance of plot in drama is not merely a historical accident. For what moves us typically is not character or idea in itself but in a particular context. Milton spoke of the meaninglessness of untried virtue; he might have said the same of untried vice or untested "truths." If characters or ideas have been "tried" for us outside the theatre, we may, of course, respond to them in the theatre as special audiences do to Passion Plays or Thanksgiving Day tableaux. But the limited appeal of such works, which assume rather than create their context, should be obvious. The great dramas seem to provide imagined contexts as independent as possible of all but the most elementary and pervasive attitudes.

Even our reactions to ethically neutral traits or objects are greatly affected by imagined contexts that imply events. A ship on the surface of the sea: exhilaration, success; that ship underwater: a sense of the tragic. We can barely imagine a drama of pure naming in which persons and ideas have no contexts by which they are qualified and judged. Hence the importance of plot in the history of drama and in understanding most plays.

In essence, plots are sequences of events. The varieties of plot have been classified in many ways, notably according to their relations to archetypal situations in myth or to variable internal characteristics. But whatever the fascinations of theory, the traditional view of plot in terms of the alterations of fortune it can present seems most practical initially. Such alterations in the fortunes of dramatic characters are called—after Aristotle— *actions*, and plots, however different from one another, can put before us only relatively few of them. Plots are like the surface of the sea, a complex of minute variations of color, texture, and direction. But actions are like the great tidal swings beneath.

To understand actions we must make distinctions among the changes in fortune that may involve the characters and then examine how these changes may be combined. The primary distinction is between *material* and *ethical* change. The most elementary actions in drama involve alterations in material circumstances—in riches, position, health. Thus the Monk in Chaucer's *Canterbury Tales* tells us:

> I wol biwaille, in manere of tragedie,
> The harm of hem that stood in heigh degree.

Reverse the case, and present: "The fortune of hem that stood in low degree," and one has the "manere of comedye."

Men can, of course, also move from innocence to guilt, and this, too, is tragic; and from sin to expiation, and this, too, is comic. But rarely do the plots of major works present changes in condition of an ethical or of a material sort alone, although so-called plays of fate are material tragedies of this kind. In any case, they are not generally as interesting as combinations in which both material and ethical fortunes alter. If both alter in the same way, we have the sort of action that, whether comic or tragic, illustrates what used to be called "poetic justice," the strange notion that the wicked are actually punished, the innocent rewarded. Such *cautionary tales* were told us in our childhood. Dylan Thomas characterizes them amusingly in a sentence about "boys who *would* skate on Farmer Giles' pond, and did, and were drowned." Quite often cautionary plays employ double actions, with poetic justice being illustrated through the fall of the sinner as well as the elevation of the deserving. Works of this sort (if they practice their naïveté well) may charm an afternoon or edify the pious, but the masterpieces of drama are not found in this category. Plays of this type are too simple to call forth the greatest artistic achievement, too naïve to touch the deepest levels of human consciousness, at which each action and passion is so intertwined with its opposite as to make poetic justice impossible.

The more complicated actions which underlie the greatest dramas are of several sorts. The simplest is *irony* or *satire*, in which material good fortune accompanies increasing wickedness. The success of the bad, as it emphasizes the folly which permits that success, is satire; as it emphasizes the vice which achieves the success, it is ironic.

In irony the conflict between a tainted innocence (gullibility) and a mitigated wickedness is external. We may speak of this wickedness as mitigated, for the successful bad characters of ironic actions typically have an impressive trait, such as superior intellect or imagination, which promotes their success. And we may call the conflict external as it is embodied in two different characters. But in the great comedies and tragedies, such as *Twelfth Night* or *Oedipus,* the conflict is internalized. The result is a comedy in which men seem to blunder their way to a success they have not quite earned, or a tragedy in which men face the consequences of their deeds in such a way as to seem not to deserve them. The complexity of this kind of comic or tragic action is best understood if we call it reflexive—that is, an action which affects the agent. Thus Oedipus thinks that he is hunting down the unknown sinner who has brought a plague on Thebes. And so he is, but his quarry is actually himself. And thus the lovers in comedy typically imagine that they are struggling against external circumstances which keep them apart. And so they are, but they are also struggling against their own ignorance, due either to the blinding effects of their passion or to comic conventions (such as mistaken identity) which represent that blindness. The reflexive actions in such comedies and tragedies typically result in ethical growth for the central figures, for in a world where innocence is impossible, self-knowledge is the essential virtue. It is essential, at any rate, for the expiation of both crime and folly. In the sorts of comic and tragic plots we are describing, self-knowledge typically occurs after a reversal in material fortune. Thus, in tragedy, Oedipus learns who he is when his efforts to identify the unknown doer of evil lead to the revelation of his own crimes. His efforts, apparently moving toward success, succeed disastrously. In comedy, the comic hero on the verge of failure often sees his situation change suddenly for the better and thus realizes that his previous efforts were in part wasted due to a self-defeating ignorance. These complex tragic and comic actions can be simply though crudely represented:

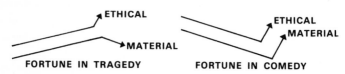

However, reversals of material fortune may be unaccompanied by insight on the part of the characters. The actions are then properly termed *pathetic*, as is the case with Romeo and Juliet, who are unaware of the extent to which their own behavior (however prompted by their family feud) led directly to disaster. Thus Romeo's death is a result of his ignorance of how Juliet had planned to bring about their success by taking a sleeping potion and thus avoiding an unwelcome marriage to Paris. Of characters in pathetic actions we use the common expression: "They never knew what hit them." But the heroes of complex tragic and comic drama do know, and that is their particular splendor.

Complex actions promise excellence in plot construction more than do the simple actions discussed earlier. In plots of simple action there may be a progression of events toward a climax at which the ultimate fortunes of the characters are decided. These events may serve one of two purposes: to define the power or weakness of opposing characters or to eliminate possible alternatives to the decisive confrontation at the climax. Thus one scene may present a mustering of attackers; another a storm which prevents the defenders from escaping by sea.

The complex action, however, is more difficult to plot, for its events must not only define powers and eliminate alternatives, they must distribute information so that the events embody dramatic irony. That is, the events must frequently imply one thing (success or failure against an external opponent) to the characters who initiate them and another thing (the characters' success or failure in self-discovery) to the audience. For simple actions the dramatist need not employ and control multiple meanings; the author of complex drama must devise a series of calculated ironic events. His rewards come from executing a more difficult task. Among them are the intensity and freedom from arbitrariness that attends the climax and the awesomeness of the self-discovery that follows. Plots of simple action fall more easily into the vice of a pat or merely expected climax followed by a denouement (literally an untieing) with only thin significance.

Yet considerable skill may be exercised in constructing the plots of simple actions. For example, there can be a pleasing and significant variation in verbal or emotional quality from one event to the next, and the action may be carried forward by a discontinuous method (as in the novels of Dickens), with successive events involving different character groups. There is something to be gained, especially in comedy, by this exchange of intensity in focus on a single group of characters for the possibility of intrigue among several groups. A further step toward virtuosity in plot construction occurs if the discontinuous presentation of events resolves into a main plot and an accompanying subplot whose function is to clarify and enrich the main plot either through ironic or thematic contrasts. The most brilliant example of both kinds of contrast is to be found in Shakespeare's *Henry IV, Part I,* in which the comic subplot involving Falstaff presents ironic contrasts to the councils of the rebels and ironic illuminations of the play's "official" values in the main plot. In this play the intertwining of events is so cunning that one hesitates to call any fraction a mere subplot.

Yet another level in the art of construction is to be found in those plots which use all or most of the characters not only as subordinates to the chief characters but as chief agents in their own stories, which form analogues—whether parallel or divergent—to the main action. Again, the best example of this may be drawn from Shakespeare. In *King Lear* it is not only Lear himself who is involved in a tragic action whereby he dies after having at last understood himself and his situation. Other characters in the play also move through suffering to understanding. And one of them, Edgar, exhibits an analogous action that goes even beyond Lear's, for Edgar's insight leads beyond misery to a capacity to rule the kingdom. His story is almost a comic analogy to Lear's tragic fate. Some of these options in plot construction may be employed for simple as well as complex actions. But generally only complex actions employ the most sophisticated plots, for only complex actions penetrate to the depths of experience that demand and support such subtlety.

The history of drama demonstrates that actions in which there is both a reversal of material fortune and a subsequent insight afford the greatest opportunities for artistic excellence. But, more important, such plays express the substance of our hopes and fears: through tragedy, the fear that the very best we can achieve—self-knowledge—we can achieve only through disaster; and through comedy, the hope that somehow we will not have to pay that price but will, like the heroes of comedy, blunder into self-knowledge and happiness at once.

OTHER PLOTS

Despite the importance of action in most of the plays that have become part of Literature, there are many plays in which the great tidal movements of fortune do not exist at all or are barely visible beneath the surface of plot. If we go to the theatre to see a play, we go also to see a "show." Spectacle—the miming of actors, the motionless presences of the set—are attractive and significant in themselves. Drama reduced to spectacle tends to stress the environmental, the contingent aspects of existence. It is no accident that farce and naturalist drama, both of which severely limit the exercise of will on the part of characters, tend toward pure mime, though farce is balletic and highly stylized, and naturalist drama strives to be as faithful to "the way things are" as possible. As Jean Piaget, the psychologist of childhood, demonstrates, we mime our reactions before we can speak them. And the primal appeal of the mimetic, which drew Victorians to opulent Christmas pantomimes, draws us to an evening among the junkies or marines in the guardhouse.[8]

At the other extreme—again de-emphasizing alterations in fortune—drama may free itself from the world of contingencies typically implied in mime and spectacle and provide us with a world of pure discourse. The great popularity of the Hell scenes from Shaw's *Man and Superman*, performed by almost motionless actors on a bare stage, demonstrates the continuing appeal of speech freed—as it often is in Shaw—from the task of representing character or furthering action and reveling in the delights of the well-said. These extremes of drama—spectacle and discourse—give rise to their own sorts of actionless plot. But something of them is also to be found in plots of action, not only in the inevitable mingling of speech and spectacle but in the delights of wit-combat in comedy or in the moving spectacle of almost pure mime in tragedy, as when dumb shows of fate appear in *Macbeth*. Further, the subvarieties of comic and tragic drama define themselves as they emphasize will and thus tend toward speech with its free speculative play, or as they de-emphasize will and insight, thus tending toward mime with its insistence on fate and environment.[9]

8 *The Connection* and *The Guardhouse* are recent productions of the New York "Living Theater," whose name alone demonstrates its naturalist bias.

Despite the philosophical implications of this emphasis or exclusion of will, it is probably wrong to speak of philosophical views as typically underlying or embodied in dramatic plots. For if we say they *underlie* the plot, we imply that they exist prior to the writing of the play, and if we say they are *embodied* in the plot, we imply the play is built around them. Typically a play, like a statue, grows under the author's hand, slowly materializing in a medium, rather than being imposed on it according to plan, philosophical or not. But it is not unreasonable to say that we can infer a pattern of thought from a pattern of dramatic events. At one extreme, the pattern is "reasonable": either the little cosmos of the play is subject to a moral law as in plays of poetic justice, or it is subject to a social or biological "law" as in those plays which present the ironies resulting from defective societies or blind fate. At the other extreme, the pattern of thought is "paradoxical." The fate of the characters in complex comedy and tragedy, for example, is not the result of poetic justice, for Oedipus is not so wicked, nor are the lovers of comedy so good, as to wholly merit their final circumstances. But they are not such pawns as to warrant our saying that their fates are merely thrust upon them. The contemporary theologian, Paul Tillich, speaks of complex tragedy as "fate plus responsibility." Perhaps this paradox will satisfy neither the moralist nor the logician. But the exploration of what eludes the canons of morality and the categories of logic is the special province of art. In this instance the special is not the esoteric, for the common life also eludes the canons and the categories. Like the protagonists of comedy and tragedy, we too are neither slaves nor masters. We cannot will away our death, but before it is upon us we can do some little things and perhaps some great ones. And what we cannot affect, we can, in part, master in understanding. In the world's great dramas we explore something of humanity's manyness of voices and something of the paradox in which it acts.

9   The varieties of drama are usefully discussed in Northrop Frye's *Anatomy of Criticism* (Princeton, N.J.: Princeton University Press, 1957), pp. 282 ff.

ll beginnings are diffi-
cult—so runs the German aphorism. Perhaps beginnings are
peculiarly difficult in German, where the verb must be delayed
until its subject is forgotten. But beginnings in understanding
a literary work in any language are difficult because plays,
poems, and stories follow the "logic of the imagination" rather
than the logic of argument or of the mechanical sequences of
time, place, and quantity. In logical argument the last statement depends upon the first, but the first statement should be
clear in itself and, wherever possible, independent of logically
prior statements. In imaginative works, however, the first passage may be obscure without the last, or the work may move
from what seems to be clear to something that, if not obscure,
is problematical or conditional.

LITERATURE AND LOGICAL ARGUMENT

Two examples will make this contrast of literature with
logical argument more concrete. We do not know fully what the
narrator of Ford Madox Ford's novel *The Good Soldier* means by
his apparently clear opening remark: "This is the saddest story
I have ever heard." We do not know what the statement means
to the man who says it, or what it ought to mean to us, until the
novel is well along. It is only then that we begin to understand
that the *saddest story* is the narrator's own story, and that his saying that it is a story he *heard*—his distant way of speaking about

it—is a sign of the very qualities which insured that his tragedy would occur. The clarity of his opening statement is deceptive, and far from merely being at the "beginning" of the work, the statement relates to all of the work—what is being built, rather than something built upon.

A second instance: Chaucer's description of the Prioress in the General Prologue to *The Canterbury Tales* sparkles with very clear physical details, but at the end of the description we do not know whether to see the Prioress as a woman who takes her religious role lightly, as a woman who combines spirituality with an admirable femininity, or as perhaps something of both. Literary works are more like rings than like rods, and the epic formula on which the greatest of them were written was that the author ought to "begin in the middle of things."

All this is by way of denial that there is any single point at which the careful consideration of any and every work must begin. Even Samuel Johnson's statement that "Particulars are not to be examined till the whole has been surveyed," should be taken as good advice rather than infallible rule. Obviously, the whole is created through its particulars, and sometimes our difficulties in understanding particulars must be clarified lest we misunderstand the whole. The process we go through in analyzing a work involves both Johnson's suggestion and its opposite. Whether we begin with a consideration of the whole or with a consideration of one or another of its parts, we must move back and forth between them until we have reconciled as fully as possible the clearest understanding we can get of both. In this process we duplicate the actual labor of the author, who attempts to provide us with

> such delight from the whole as is compatible with a distinct gratification from each component part.

This description of Coleridge's (in *Biographia Literaria*, XIV) has a cold, intellectualistic ring which promises less than the *delight* it identifies as the goal of the writer's—and the reader's —effort. Perhaps we should temper Coleridge's tone with something Keats wrote in a letter of May 3, 1818, to J. H. Reynolds:

> We read fine things but never feel them to the full until we have gone the same steps as the author.

FINDING AN ACCURATE TEXT

Obviously, readers and writers do not go through the same steps in precisely the same order. The writer's last step is, or ought to be, the reader's first. When he has completed his work, the writer tries to make certain that it is published in the form he intended. And the reader's first step ought to be to discover if this has been done. Many editions, even "standard" editions, of major authors are simply not to be trusted.

A great American scholar and critic was betrayed into making an imaginative but irrelevant observation about the ethical import of *Moby Dick* because of a misprint that had altered Melville's original from "coiled fish" to "soiled fish." One wonders what more horrendous results have come from the publishing farce involving two transposed chapters in Henry James' novel *The Ambassadors*. The first American edition inverted the order of Chapters 28 and 29. The first English edition got the order right, but since that time (despite the triumphant predictions of publishing houses) *The Ambassadors* has appeared in edition after edition with the initial error uncorrected. There are correct editions available in paperback, but perhaps as many erroneous copies as correct ones are in the hands of readers.

These, however, are relatively simple matters. More complicated problems arise when a writer corrects or emends his work from one edition to another without indicating which versions are to be preferred, when a writer cannot or does not supervise the proofreading of his work (death, fashion, and literary piracy are the common causes here), or when an editor simply takes it on himself to silently emend the author's work. Imagine how far astray the reader may go when he fails to note the difference between the earlier and later editions of the poems of Wordsworth, when he reads pirated versions of Joyce's *Ulysses*, or when he reads the editorial work of that defender of morality who provided the public with:

Give me a wench above thirteen
Already voted to the Queen
Of Love and Lovers

instead of the seventeenth-century original:

Give me a wench about thirteene
Already voted to the Queene
Of lust and lovers.

The older the work one reads, the more care one must take in finding a faithful and well-annotated text. Older methods of printing, with their handset type, their uncertain proofreading, their relatively greater variety of printing house and compositor eccentricities, frequently resulted in editions whose unreliability we are just beginning to appreciate fully. The relatively new branches of literary scholarship, "analytic" and "critical" bibliography, whose most impressive achievement to date is Charlton Hinman's work on *The Printing and Proof-Reading of the First Folio of Shakespeare,* allow us to see how far we are from a completely reliable text of even the greatest of English poets. Yet it is going too far to dismiss all literary criticism and even reading itself as founded on sands of misprint and bad editions. Of Shakespeare's works we have several good series such as the New Arden, and several excellent one-volume editions, notably those of Kittredge and Peter Alexander, though we must hope that further bibliographic investigation will result in editions that depend less on the taste and learning of editors and more on the facts of the Elizabethan printshop. In any case, there is little excuse for the student's using any but the best current edition of his author.

Often the instructor will be able to help here, often the librarian. But the student himself can discover the best edition of his author through an hour's work in the library consulting reviews of editions in scholarly journals. The results are often amusing and have the exhilarating effect of puncturing delusions about the sacredness of the printed page. Another hour spent comparing a college anthology version of a poem or play with the version in the best edition may, in a few instances, be even more instructive and can develop the tough-mindedness about detail indispensable to literary study.

READING FOR THE PATTERN: PROMISE AND PERFORMANCE

But suppose one has one's good text. The next step that the reader must take is one that would be fatal for a writer, that is, a wholly sympathetic reading. The writer—aiming at nothing less than an impossible perfection—can never afford to view his own work this way, and typically, when it is in print, he ignores his brain-child or views it with anguish. But the reader, unaware of the disappointing gap between hope and achievement, must attend sympathetically to success and failure on the actual page, and his attention is the measure of his sympathy. Henry James' advice to writers—"Be one of those on whom nothing is lost"—is equally advice to readers.

But on all of us something will be lost. "Homer nods" and so do we. What one actually *gets* in a first reading varies enormously with the reader and the occasions on which he reads. But on successive readings there should emerge that sense of the whole and that sense of particulars which literary analysis attempts to refine and reconcile.

Prior to both, however, we ought to try to grasp the design of the work, the pattern of promise and performance on which the particulars and the whole alike depend. In the lyric "To Juan at the Winter Solstice," the poet and novelist Robert Graves begins:

> There is one story and one story only
> That will prove worth your telling,

and concludes with the line:

> But nothing promised that is not performed.[1]

The lines are suggestive of the essential literary compact. Everything the writer does is a promise. If he titles his work *The Tragedie of King Richard the Second,* he promises us that the work will be tragic and about that king, unless his title, like Fielding's *The Tragedy of Tragedies* (first titled *Tom Thumb*) is facetious, in which case the writer must be true to his promise to be facetious. If a poem begins in a five-stress line, the writer has promised that it will continue so, though his writing at all is a promise that he will repay our attention with something better than un-

1   From *Collected Poems* by Robert Graves. Reprinted with the permission of International Authors N.V.

varied, metronomic repetition of his meter. Further, the poet's subject matter involves promises, too, and fulfilling them may require a change to other meters entirely, as it does in the songs in Shakespeare's plays, or in the various sections of T. S. Eliot's *The Waste Land*. The reader's most important business is to identify the writer's promises and to attend to how they are performed.

For his part, the writer must honor both his general promise to write well and the specific obligations he undertakes when he makes the promises of this or that incident or character or style. From these two sorts of obligation there emerges a standard by which the reader can judge the forward flow of the work, for the writer must not only present us with performances but with performances of literary excellence.

To continue the five-beat line monotonously, to present an incident that is merely predictable, a tragedy that follows formula, to use a language of cliché, is perhaps to honor the specific obligations but not the general one. What the reader must sense in the flow of the work is whether or not the promises it makes are performed in a way that seems surprising as it happens yet, on reflection, inevitable: *inevitable* because the performance is what the specific promise requires, yet *surprising* for surprise—rather than dullness—is what the writer's general promise requires. Aristotle, writing of excellence in the plot of tragedy (*Poetics*, 1452 a, S. H. Butcher, trans.), says that its effect "is best produced when the events come on us by surprise; and the effect is heightened when, at the same time, they follow as cause and effect." This is a particularization of the excellence possible in plot. But the same principle—the excellence of the surprisingly inevitable—may be found in characterization, diction, and the other elements of literary works. Again, illustrations are instructive.

As Kenneth Burke has brilliantly pointed out in his essay "Psychology and Form" (reprinted in his *Counter-Statement*, 1931), we expect and expect and expect the appearance of the Ghost in *Hamlet* because he has been promised to us through the conversations of Horatio and the palace guards; but when at last the Ghost does appear, we are surprised because Shakespeare has, just before the appearance, teased our attention elsewhere with talk about drinking in Denmark and with Hamlet's comments on human frailty. Yet these comments are not mere filler, red herrings drawn across the Ghost's trail. They, too, are promises—for we expect to see more of the vices of the Danes, to hear more from Hamlet on human frailty; and they are also performances, for we were promised, during the earlier scenes at court, something more about Hamlet's view of the king and his style of government, and this promise Hamlet's speech in part performs.

The foregoing analysis suggests a focus for the reader's attention. In the forward flow of the work we look for its promises, then for whether they are fulfilled at all, and for whether or not they are fulfilled with literary virtuosity—what Aristotle calls literally "wondrousness"—and then, finally, for whether various promises and performances are related to one another with economy. When we say a work is excellent, we mean that it does these things.

A work may, of course, fail. It may promise too little or make its promises vaguely. It may not fulfill its promises, as when plot wanders or language is inadequate to what it ought to express. It may perform what is not promised, as when in Act V the villain, for no discernible reason, turns saint. It may perform its promises too quickly, before we have developed sufficient concern with them to be pleased by the fulfillment of our expectations. Or it may perform its promises dully: a checkerboard is not an exciting design.

The relations between promise and performance are obviously various. They are made more complex still by the requirement that performance be not merely perfunctory but artistically excellent. We only complicate our problem as readers by attempting to view excellence in literature as something dependent on the reader's state of mind. The virtuosity or "wondrousness" of good literary performance exists in the work itself, and the reader must be attentive and informed in order to be able to react to it. The example of how Shakespeare presents Hamlet's Ghost seems to illustrate how the writer plays with the audience's "psychology," specifically with its capacity for being distracted. But if we examine other examples of successful patterns of promise and performance, we will see that they depend on the reader's knowledge and on his capacity for *not* being distracted. (We may, of course, even say this about the Ghost example. If

we had not attended to Hamlet's remarks on Danish alcohol-
ism, the Ghost's appearance would have been no surprise.)
Again, examples will concretize what is meant by specifically
literary expectations and by the knowledge and attention they
require if we are to appreciate the excellence of the writer's
performance.

The primary knowledge the reader requires before he can
appreciate virtuosity of performance in language is a knowledge
of language itself—specifically of metrics and of what used to be
called Rhetoric before the false identification of cultivated speech
with dishonesty or snobbishness made rhetoric a term of abuse.
One can understand the artistry possible in metrical or rhetorical performance by examining passages in which the writer
employs metrical or rhetorical patterns which he interrupts or
terminates in an unexpected fashion in order to achieve a promised significance. Perhaps the clearest instances are metrical,
because meter, with its regular alternation of heavily accented
and lightly accented syllables, most clearly sets up a pattern
and thus allows us to respond to deviations.

A famous instance of metrical virtuosity occurs in John
Donne's poem "The Good Morrow," a variation on the aubade.
The aubade, a form frequent in the poetry of the medieval trou-
badours, was a song sung by lovers forced to part at sunrise.
Donne plays with the aubade conventions, substituting a conversational and realistic tone for its traditional lyricism, and the
mutual illumination of the lovers' discovery of their love for the
physical rising of the sun. "The Good Morrow" is thus at once
a more realistic and a more idealized view of love than one gets
from the traditional aubade. Part of the effect of realism depends on Donne's handling of meter. The poem is written in
iambic pentameter lines, that is, lines of ten syllables which are
alternately lightly and heavily stressed, the even-numbered syllables receiving the heavy stress. The poem opens with a question spoken by the lover:

> I wonder by my troth what thou and I
> Did, till we loved?

In the first line the pattern of alternating light and heavy stresses is loosely followed, but toward its end, the words *troth, thou* and *I* are stressed sufficiently for us to feel the iambic rhythm quite clearly. Therefore we are led to expect that the second line will begin with an unaccented syllable. But it does not. Instead, the stress pattern of the first two syllables of the second line is reversed and we are given a trochee (a heavily stressed syllable followed by a lightly stressed one), and this is followed by the two rather heavily stressed syllables in *we loved,* which serve to emphasize Donne's earlier departure from the expected iambic rhythm. We are forced to read the lines:

> what thou and I
> DID till we loved?

It is as though the wonderment of love had broken through the artificialities of meter into the passion of direct speech. Donne has set up and allowed us to *expect* the iambic norm in order to violate it. Donne's contemporary, Ben Jonson, said that Donne ought to be hanged for "not keeping the accent," for metrical irregularity. But for this interruption of the iambic pattern one wants to give Donne the highest praise. The line is still recognizable iambic pentameter, but Donne has managed to wrest from it the passion his subject demands and the conversational realism appropriate to the particular character of the poem's fictive lover. All this is the result of Donne's setting up a specific metrical *expectation* and then interrupting it in an unexpected way. But unless we are informed about meter and attentive to it we miss the poet's art.

Chaucer surprises us delightfully in the General Prologue to *The Canterbury Tales* by doing with subject matter what Donne does with meter. The first nineteen lines of the prologue comprise a single sentence. They begin with an elaborate description of the coming of spring. This description is highly conventional, apparently very little different from the pattern of springtime detail that opens innumerable medieval poems. The drought ends, the buds appear, the zephyrs come. But after he has told us about how even the birds sleep open-eyed because of the stimulus of reawakened nature to their *corages,* Chaucer does not continue with the romantic or the heroic events his lines have *prepared* for. The word *corages* (heart, disposition, desire) rhymes with *pilgrimages*. With a half-smile, Chaucer tells us that in the spring the human fancy lightly turns to thoughts of— piety. The marvelous comic realism here is lost on us if we are inattentive or if we know nothing of the literary conventions relating to descriptions of spring in chronicle, romance, and lyric.

A more complex example, involving virtuosity in diction, is to be found in Blake's poem "London." It can be presented most clearly if we invent an alternative that Blake did not employ (Version A) and contrast it with the actual (Version B) lines of the poem. The contrast involves a single word, the last in both versions.

> A. But most thro' midnight streets I hear
>   How the youthful harlot's curse
>   Blasts the new-born infant's ear.

> B. But most thro' midnight streets I hear
>   How the youthful harlot's curse
>   Blasts the new-born infant's tear.

The difference between *tear* and *ear* is the difference between distinguished and merely adequate verse. The preceding lines promise us something momentous and significant through the words *most* and *midnight,* and through the cue that we are to observe the effects not of any curse, but of the curse of a *youthful* harlot. Yet Version A gives us only description. The curse, like any unpleasant street noise, is offensive to the *ear;* it has no greater significance. It merely completes in a commonplace fashion the pattern of aural words: hear-curse-blasts-ear.

But in Blake's actual version the aural pattern of hear-curse-blasts ends not as one might expect, but with the word *tear.* The line is no longer a piece of physical description. It takes on a larger significance, for the curse now *blasts* not only in the physical sense, but *blasts* in the sense of blighting and withering all the pain and promise of infancy. Blake's version, Version B, is a gloss on Yeats' lament that "everywhere the ceremony of innocence is drowned." The inertia of the aural pattern hear-curse-blasts-ear is increased by the obviousness of *ear* as a rhyme for *hear.* But Blake resists inertia in rhyme and diction, and the result is excellence: a surprising, yet inevitable, turn in diction and meaning that satisfies the rhyme scheme and the demands of the poem's subject.

This last was an example of how the poet works with and against the inertia of language—its tendency to keep moving in certain directions. And it may be argued that much of what can be known about these directions of language (usage) is *common* knowledge. Perhaps. But there is nothing so difficult to grasp as the obvious, and the very presence of inertia in language—of cliché, *normal* syntax, *fashionable* speech—is a convenience gained at the cost of blunted or discontinuous awareness. Commonplace language is precisely what we become *un*aware of. Moreover, the norms change with time. "All hell broke loose" was not a cliché when Milton used it in *Paradise Lost*. And norms of language change also with place and social station. The good reader must have a trained sense of such alterations.

The next example requires an awareness of language conventions, but it will illustrate the same principle in the upsetting of the "expected" word order that Blake's "London" illustrates in the upsetting of the "expected" directions of diction and rhyme. John O'Hara, the contemporary American fiction writer, has a remarkable ear for American speech, not only for how it goes, but for how it goes under pressure. His short story "Graven Image" (*The New Yorker,* March 6, 1943) shows this sensitivity to good advantage. The story deals with individual ambition and social status, and with how poorly they harmonize with the American tradition and hope for an egalitarian democracy. This "theme" of the story is presented, of course, in plot and characterization. But it is also presented with great virtuosity through the way in which at critical points O'Hara's language conforms not to the expectations of *normal* sentence order, but to his promises that the language will satisfy the specific demands of the theme and the general obligation of literary art. Quite early in the story, the Under-Secretary in a *liberal* administration—a short man who wears his role uneasily—tells his chauffeur to park in front of a busy hotel entrance.

"Will the Under-Secretary be here long?" asked the doorman.

"Why?" said the little man.

"Because if you were going to be here, sir, only a short while, I'd let your man leave the car here, at the head of the rank."

"Leave it there *anyway,*" said the Under-Secretary.

This exchange has some crudities. The phrase *little man* is heavy-handed; it stacks the cards against the Under-Secretary and (because the detail is too "pat") artlessly *tells* us what it ought to *show* us. But contrast this artlessness with O'Hara's virtuosity in the doorman's reply to the Under-Secretary's question. Look especially at the placement of the word *sir.* It is precisely *not* at those points in the sentence at which our knowledge of current speech would lead us to expect it. It does not come after *Because,* or after *while,* or at the end of the sentence. It comes at a very awkward interruption in the flow of the sentence, and its awkwardness shows us the care and discomfort of the doorman in addressing the Under-Secretary, shows us something of the character of the *little* man who imposes such discomfort, and thus performs the promise made in the social theme of the story. In this passage, O'Hara fails unimportantly with one stroke and succeeds brilliantly with another. The failure results from too obvious a fulfillment of the promise to give us a *small* man who worships a graven image. The success comes from an artful interruption of the conventional course of the sentence to fulfill the promise of the theme in an unexpected way.

Perhaps the most common rhetorical excellences in literature are brevity and its conjunct, precision. Brevity and precision in language are surprising, for if we know anything about how language is generally employed, we know that it is diffuse and vague. The poet Auden could define his art as "memorable speech" only because most speech is not. The brief exactitude shines like a nugget against the uncultivated common acres of language. Its achievement is perhaps at the center of literary art. When Shakespeare called brevity "the soul of wit" he used *wit* in a larger meaning than the current one. And the German word *dichten* means not only "to write poetry" but "to make close or tight."

Thus one finds almost everywhere in Shakespeare the shock of brevity coupled with exactness that contrasts so sharply with

our experience of the vagueness and length of ordinary discourse. Two examples from the opening scene of *Hamlet* will
serve to clarify our point. Shakespeare in this first scene must
put before us two sorts of character: the honest, perceptive,
simple soldier like Marcellus; and Horatio, the Stoical, not
easily convinced intellectual. Marcellus he must present rapidly;
Horatio appears throughout the play. These two sorts of persons
must be presented because the composition of a drama implies
a promise to present characters who speak differently—in their
own right. Moreover, the particular tragic action in *Hamlet* requires a basis in individuality for the false estimates that complicate relations among characters in the play. Finally, the different attitudes of Marcellus and Horatio intensify our doubts
(and our certainties) about the Ghost. Thus the Ghost and the
realm of Denmark may become as problematical as they must
be if we are to appreciate Hamlet's doubts about them.

But see how Shakespeare introduces Horatio:

BERNARDO: Say,
    What, is Horatio there?

HORATIO: A piece of him.

In four words we get the wit and intelligence of the man,
the skepticism about appearances, the idealism that finds earthly
existence only *a piece* of man—in short, almost everything that
Horatio is to become throughout the play. But four lines later
Marcellus presents his own "epiphany" or brief revelation.
Speaking of the Ghost, Marcellus says:

    Horatio says 'tis but our fantasy,
    And will not let belief take hold of him.

Note here the unpredictable phrasing of the second line. Characters in Shakespeare may resolve to believe something against
evidence, but like most of us they generally try to reach beliefs
on the basis of evidence and test. So does Marcellus. But belief
here has apparently *taken hold* of him. This indicates, first, the
intensity of his experience on seeing the Ghost, and second, that
he is one in whom, unlike Horatio, the rational process is not

central, and so belief may be described by him in language that makes it seem external, something that takes hold from the outside.

In the preceding examples we have tried to particularize what we mean by saying that the successful work performs what it promises in a way that is excellent because it is surprising, because its language upsets the dullness of merely commonplace or expected patterns. Reflecting on these examples, one must conclude that the successful work does not merely play with the "psychology" of the reader. It depends quite often on the reader's understanding of the conventional patterns of language and of literary form, patterns which the writer exploits through violating or transcending them, thus defeating dullness. Obviously, then, if we are to understand literature, that is, analyze its form and react to its excellence, we must have something more than a human "psychology." We must have a specific understanding of the conventions of language, of the norms of expression at various times and places, and of how rhetorical devices usually work. And we must have an understanding of the larger conventions of different literary forms. Unfortunately, formal schooling in rhetoric and in literary forms decayed rapidly after the Renaissance. But good modern literary training and the self-training of extensive and attentive reading in the major authors can more than make up the loss.

Reflection on the examples cited may give us some clearer view of the social uses of literature and literary study. Custom, the philosopher Hume observed, is the great guide of life. But it can also become the great enemy of vitality. Civilization advances through the defeat of inadequate custom by insight. And learning itself—the "information" theorists seem to tell us —is but the interruption of routine. We may conclude that the precise reading of the great literary works can be civilizing in the highest degree, and that, as Aristotle said in the *Poetics,* 1448 b, the delights of literature are the delights of learning.

Sophisticated reading and analysis of literature begin when the reader can extract patterns of promise and performance from the forward motion of the work and put them to the tests of economy, complexity, and virtuosity. One cannot make good English sentences with a multiple subject like syntax-diction-imagery-rhetoric-rhythm-action-character-idea. Yet all of these and more make up the patterns of promise and performance in a work of literature. After one has got a sense of the pattern—of the fact and quality of its presence—one can attempt to characterize the whole of a given work and its particulars, employing some of the strategies suggested in earlier chapters.

WORD, REFERENCE, AND ALLUSION

Unfortunately, we cannot go directly to this attempt. Our initial sense of the pattern of a work is almost always gained through the kind of reading which, though it is attentive to details, must put certain of them aside, postponing them for the sake of an uninterrupted experience of the work. This is not due only to the laziness of refusing to leave the armchair for the dictionary, or for the longer trek to the bowels of the library itself. It is justified by the reader's obligation to the writer "to hear the man out." For once, comfort is a virtue. But after the pattern, the interest of the work, is established, we are obliged to do the "homework" that comes before more serious analysis. We must track down and puzzle out all the allusions, references, and words we have put aside. Despite the universality of literature, it is of a time and place, of a moment in the history of a language and a man. The recovery of the meaning of allusions and words is indispensable if we are to go beyond first impressions. If we have a well-annotated edition before us, the editor has done most of our work, either in footnotes, glossaries, or introductions, or in bibliographies that refer us to explications or to other works on works. But even so, it is useful to remember that perhaps the most misleading aid to serious reading is the ordinary dictionary. What one wants is an extraordinary dictionary, one that gives us the meanings of words at a given time in history. The *OED* (*Oxford English Dictionary*) is invaluable here, as are works like C. T. Onions' *Shakespeare Glossary.* They enable us to avoid the errors that come from assuming that the author's English is our own. A dictionary that records only our current usage will be inadequate, even as an aid to reading only contemporary literature. Poetry especially may employ consciously archaic diction—whether for serious or satirical effects—or may incorporate whole stretches of earlier verse, as in *The Waste Land,* whose author once said that great writers do not borrow—they rob. In addition, the language of poetry is highly conventional, charged with a richness of simultaneous meanings that may include a whole range of meanings no longer current. Current meaning, in short, is what the language of poetry abhors, because, paradoxically, what is current is not often vital, and in following the poet Pound's injunction to "make it new," the poet must sometimes make his language old.

Of allusion and reference, those clues to what extends the meaning of a work and makes a work part of its age and its author, little need be said here. One unfortunate perversion of the sound idea that a good literary work must be complete and self-consistent is the comfortable delusion that it can be correctly read by an intelligent, newly arrived Martian. Much of the "discipline" of literature is concerned with knowing when an intelligent and sensitive interpretation of a work is dead wrong: wrong because it is naïve and uninformed. The tracing of allusion and reference is a necessary route to discovering the "furniture of the mind" of a writer and an age. Hence such research not only clarifies a specific portion of a text but gradually coalesces into a general conception of an author and an age. When one traces the allusion to George III and to processes of manufacture in the phrase *german forged links* in the rough draft of Blake's poem "London," one sees not only the avoidance of merely descriptive topicality that led Blake to change the phrase to *mind-forg'd manacles*, but one gets a vivid sense of the poet's cast of mind and the politics of the era.

When the reader has grasped the pattern of a work, begun to sense its particular excellence, and traced its difficulties of language and allusion, he stands near the height on which meaningful criticism and scholarship take place.

Chapter Six

P

revious chapters have considered the major types of literary works and some of the strategies useful in understanding them. In this chapter some —though by no means all—of the distinctions and generalizations made earlier will be applied. What follows is a group of three short essays or "trials"—one on a lyric poem, one on the introductory passages from a work of fiction, and another on the opening scene of a play. These essays do not pretend to exhaust the subtleties of the passages they deal with, but they do provide some practical illustration of how one goes about making a beginning in analyzing a work.

KEATS' "WHEN I HAVE FEARS . . ."

The question of how one begins the reading of a lyric poem is somewhat different from the problem of beginning a story, a novel, or a play; for most poems of this kind are so short that almost as soon as we are "into" the poem we are "out of" it again. Of course no one should think of giving a poem only one rapid reading, as if it were a newspaper article. It is more like an object to examine than a statement merely to take in, and therefore one does not fully come to grips with the beginning of a poem without at least some sense of it as a whole. Perhaps the most important thing to be gained from a first reading— more important even, at this stage, than "what the poem is about"—is a recognition of whatever formal aspects it may have. Such factors as its division into stanzas, the rhyme scheme within each stanza, and the presence of repetition and variation often provide the key to a poem's fullest meaning. The following analysis will therefore take the poem's formal structure as a guide to comprehending those patterns of relationship that the poem comprises as an expressive totality.

Our example is a sonnet, the most common and among the most strictly defined of short lyric forms. Perhaps we should preface its discussion by suggesting that the formal confines of a sonnet make it not a cage where pent-up genius languishes but, like a billiard table, a conventionalized "area" within which a true artist can exhibit his skill at the game.

I
When I have fears that I may cease to be
    Before my pen has glean'd my teeming brain,
Before high-piled books, in charact'ry,
    Hold like rich garners the full-ripen'd grain;

II
When I behold, upon the night's starr'd face,   5
    Huge cloudy symbols of a high romance,
And think that I may never live to trace
    Their shadows, with the magic hand of chance;

III
And when I feel, fair creature of an hour,
    That I shall never look upon thee more,   10
Never have relish in the faery power
    Of unreflecting love!—then on the shore
Of the wide world I stand alone, and think
Till Love and Fame to nothingness do sink.

——*John Keats*

Keats' "When I have fears . . ." is an *Elizabethan* or *Shakespearean* sonnet: a poem consisting of fourteen lines in iambic pentameter rhymed *a b a b c d c d e f e f g g*. The rhyme scheme divides the sonnet into three alternate-rhyme quatrains and a concluding couplet. An awareness of this pattern should lead the reader to expect and look for ways it might be reflected in the organization of what the poem says. One can scarcely avoid, in fact, making the important discovery that the rhyme scheme is paralleled, or nearly so, by the syntactical pattern of the sonnet. The poem is a single sentence consisting of a series of three conditions followed by their consequence. Each quatrain is an adverbial *when* clause, and the concluding couplet contains the main clause and another subordinate clause. This characterization is not quite exact, because the main clause ("then on the shore . . .") does encroach upon the third quatrain, but a high degree of correspondence between the grammatical structure and the formal structure is nevertheless apparent.

Each of the *when* clauses describes the poet's anxiety about premature death. That, of course, is to put it very loosely. We would hope the effect of these three quatrains is not merely that of repetition. A good reader should expect the poet to have achieved some scheme respecting these three *when* clauses, some arrangement of relationships that would have the significance of *design* rather than the inconsequentiality of *reiteration*. Indeed, parallelism—certainly the dominant structural device in this poem—invites the comparison of corresponding parts to the end that meaningful, or at least satisfying, relationships will be disclosed.

Clearly quatrains I and II have to do with the *Fame* and quatrain III with the *Love* which sink to nothingness in the final couplet. The first quatrain refers to the poet's fears that death will cut short his life before his creative potentialities have been fully realized. Aptly enough, his unwritten works are likened to a harvest which, were it not for death's blight, his pen might glean at maturity. The second quatrain also expresses his fear in terms of unfulfilled powers, but here death is regarded not as an interruption of the natural and common process of growth and maturity but rather as the thwarting of a capacity to convey some sudden and secret vision. In the third quatrain the poet's sense of his mortality is expressed in the pathos of unconsummated love. As Love and Fame appear in an order of *descent* to nothingness at the conclusion, the inverse order of Fame (I and II) then Love (III) must therefore be in some sense an *ascent*. But is such a movement effectively "acted out" by the poem? Or, to put the matter differently, *ascent* and *descent* are abstractions; what, if anything, do they refer to in the poem itself?

To facilitate the discussion of this question and to point up the sonnet's structural qualities, let us schematize some of the corresponding elements in the three quatrains.

Quatrain	A	B	C	D	E
I Fame (through maturation)	have fears	(may) cease to be	has glean'd hold	charact'ry	[seasonal cycle]
II Fame (by em- bodying a vision)	behold	(may) never live	trace	magic hand (huge cloudy symbols)	night
III Love	feel	(shall) never look	have relish	faery power	hour

An examination of the poem's diction, for which the diagram above provides an outline, indicates that an ascending pattern of both intricacy and coherence is indeed evident. The vertical columns represent a series of distinct but interrelated "three-stage" progressions by which the poet's concern with mortality moves toward its climax. Column A refers to the parallel beginnings of each quatrain. Surely an "ascent" is present in the shift from "When I *have fears*" to "When I *behold*" to "And when I *feel*"—a pattern of increasing intensity. As the poet contemplates his untimely decease, his emotional involvement becomes more direct, more absorbing. To *have fears* implies a vague, generalized concern. *Behold,* in the second quatrain, is more distinct, and with the other verb in the quatrain, *think* (line 7), suggests the conjunction of perception and reflection in a still more insistent absorption in the possibility of death. *Feel,* then, in the third quatrain, climaxes the rise of intensity by introducing the most intimate and immediate level of response. The change from *having fears* to *beholding/thinking* to *feeling* is a change toward active participation, and thus the process of pondering the relation of

death to Fame and Love draws the poet (and the reader) more
fully into the experience.

This increasing intensity is also reflected by the degree of
vividness with which the conception of death is expressed in
each quatrain. The relevant phrases are those in column B. "I
may *cease to be*" in the first quatrain has a certain euphemistic
delicacy; "I may *never live*" (II) is more bald but still somewhat
abstract. In III *may* changes to *shall,* and the terms for mortal
extinction are correspondingly definite: "I shall *never look . . .
never have relish.* . . ." To die is to lose forever the delight of sensory experience. As death is thus becoming more real, the life
it extinguishes is also imagined in terms increasingly vivid and
active—terms listed in column C. The poet's existence is represented in quatrain I, through a kind of metonymy, only by the
high-piled books that *hold* the products of his creation. In quatrain II we have the poet longing *to trace* his visions "with the
magic hand of chance"; he is both present and active to a
degree he was not in the first quatrain. But such *tracing,* not
altogether free from connotations of the dutiful and the method-
ical, is several degrees less intense than to *have relish,* which we
find to be the corresponding notion in quatrain III.

As one's sense of a general progression of intensity in the
diction of the first twelve lines becomes clearer, more of the
poem's elements are seen to fit this pattern and enrich it. *Charact'ry, magic hand,* and *faery power*—the items in column D—all
refer to some form and degree of the creative or actualizing
force, whatever one wishes to call the vital principle whose tran-
sience the poet so keenly feels. In the first quatrain written words
—*charact'ry*—embody and preserve the thoughts and sensations
of the poet. Here—and in view of the imagery of natural growth
and maturation it is fitting—the term carries little suggestion
of the occult or supernatural, which the corresponding words
in the subsequent quatrains clearly denote. Yet *charactery* does
emphasize the *symbolizing* power of language, a power which
we take for granted but which is given something like its due
in magic spells and incantations. Artistic creation, or Fame, is
more intensely conceived in the second quatrain. It is no longer
a kind of fruition or a mental harvest; it is the recording of a
tenebrous vision by "the magic hand of chance"—that form of
automatic writing traditionally associated with poetic inspira-

tion. Thus the shift from *charact'ry* to *huge cloudy symbols* appropriately marks a heightening of the mystery and an enlargement of its scope.

As Love is more intense and more fulfilling than Fame, its powers are endowed in the poem with a more purely supernatural, more ethereal quality. Spirit may be incarnated in *high-piled books,* but it is relatively inert. Magic (II) may mediate between the natural and supernatural, but the poet-magician is subject to *chance* and can at best only trace the shadows of symbols (as Plato thought poets to be but imitators of imitations). The ecstasy of love, however, is the thing itself, as most poets admit by so often writing about it.

In the course of its elaboration of mortal fears, the sonnet makes life's powers and pleasures seem increasingly wonderful. There is, of course, a psychological truth in this—a truth that underlies another aspect of the relationship between the three quatrains. This aspect might be called the shifting *temporal context,* and it is represented—quite inadequately—by column E. As death becomes more real and life more dear, time's presence is emphasized and its very brevity is more strongly felt. Something like this is what occurs in the sonnet. The frame of reference in the first quatrain, submerged in the imagery of maturity and harvest, is the seasonal cycle, to which life is implicitly likened. In the second it is the diurnal round that is suggested by "the *night's* starr'd face." Finally, this intensifying contraction of the temporal context culminates in the poet's reference to his beloved as "fair creature of an *hour.*"

Our diagram has now exhausted its usefulness; the various lines of development it illustrates fuse in the sonnet itself to form a single movement. Its climax is the phrase *unreflecting love* (line 12). The epithet *unreflecting* is calculated to arrest our notice, to challenge our sensitivity, and all that has been observed about the sonnet thus far argues the particular appropriateness of the word. Love stands in the poem as the pinnacle of mortal existence, the ultimate goal toward which the poet's fears that he may cease to be lead his anxious longing. That such love is *unreflecting* indicates the senses in which this is so. The word suggests, in one area of its meaning, the spontaneous and immediate, the intense and ecstatic; in another more fundamental sense it characterizes love as something whose function is not to contain, represent, or image forth another thing but rather to serve its own direct ends, something which—in contradistinction to the implications of *gleaning* and *holding* (I) or *tracing* (II) —has no object other than itself.

The course of the poem from this point of emotional intensity to the conclusion is a falling away, a sinking from the *all* of unreflecting love to the *nothingness* in line 14. Is it a flaw in the structural neatness of the sonnet that what we have called its climax does not come precisely at the end of line 12? No doubt the answer will vary with each reader's sense of form, but several points can be made in defense of this slight disalignment of the poem's rhetorical-emotional pattern and its rhyme scheme. For one thing, the concluding couplet is a potential awkwardness in the Elizabethan sonnet form. After the series of three quatrains, with their numberless possibilities for interesting and effective relationship, the couplet comes as a kind of "tail" (the Italian for "tail," *coda*, refers to the analogous effect in music). One has only to read a fair sampling of Shakespeare's sonnets to realize that even that supreme master was not always successful in making the final couplet a really effective conclusion and not merely an afterthought. Anything that tends to stress the separateness of the couplet increases the likelihood of its seeming a lame addition to a twelve-line, three-stanza poem. The sonnet we are examining has, as it is, so many elements which emphasize its three-quatrain division that perhaps Keats did well not to break the thought precisely between these quatrains and the last two lines.

So much for a strictly formal justification. A more "internal" one has to do with the effect of transition and with the poem's total meaning. The relationship between the imaginative ascent to *unreflecting love* and the descent to *nothingness* appears to be rather complex psychologically. When the poet says "—then on the shore . . . ," he means *then* not only in the sense of mere succession (When I had studied in the library, *then* I went swimming), but also in the sense of *consequence* (When I had heard him play, *then* I could appreciate jazz). It is as if the descent to nothingness not only follows but *grows out of* the ascent to unreflecting love. Thus a modulation from the one to the other is better represented by a carry-over from quatrains to couplet than by an emphatic break between them.

At the moment of poise before Love and Fame sink to nothingness, the poet is, imaginatively, indeed "on the shore/ Of the wide world." His mingled sense of life as both precarious and sweet has led him to the rapturous ideal of unreflecting love. Fear and desire can go no further. As both the rhyme and the reason of the final couplet would urge, the crucial word in the subsequent sinking to nothingness is *think* (line 13). Readers familiar with Keats might at this point bring to bear upon their understanding of the poem the famous exclamation from one of his letters, "O for a Life of Sensations rather than of Thoughts!" and the aphoristic line from the poem *Lamia,* " . . . a moment's thought is passion's passing bell"; but as a matter of fact no gloss from the poet's other works is really needed here. We respond to the significance of the word *think* from our awareness—gained *within* the poem—of unreflecting love as the very antithesis of thought.

Thus Love and Fame dwindle to nothingness in the face of the poet's solitary and searching thoughts. But how are we to feel about such a conclusion? It is not actual experiences of love and fame that disintegrate, but rather the poet's *conception* of these two essences in all their desirable improbability. Therefore, this sinking to nothingness might be regarded as a release from the tyranny of a futile longing. But then again, if such release is a consolation, it may be a bitter one, purchased at the sacrifice of an intensity of feeling. We cannot resolve the matter by (in Keats' own words) "any irritable reaching after fact and reason." The poem concerns an experience that is, like most human experiences of some poignancy, a complex mixture of pleasure and hurt, the proportions of which seem to change each time it is recalled. Perhaps that is why, as thoroughly as we may study the poem and as well as we may think we know it, there will always be reason to go back to it and begin our experience of it anew.

GULLIVER'S TRAVELS

THE GULLIVER-SYMPSON CORRESPONDENCE

A Letter from Capt. Gulliver, to His Cousin Sympson

I hope you will be ready to own publickly, whenever you shall be called to it, that by your great and frequent Urgency you prevailed on me to publish a very loose and uncorrect Account of my Travels; with Direction to hire some young Gentlemen of either University to put them in Order, and correct the Style, as my Cousin *Dampier* did by my Advice, in his Book called, *A Voyage round the World.* But I do not remember I gave you Power to consent that any thing should be omitted, and much less that any thing should be inserted: Therefore, as to the latter, I do here renounce every thing of that Kind; particularly a Paragraph about her Majesty the late Queen *Anne,* of most pious and glorious Memory; although I did reverence and esteem her more than any of human Species. But you, or your Interpolator, ought to have considered, that as it was not my Inclination, so was it not decent to praise any Animal of our Composition before my Master *Houyhnhnm:* And besides, the Fact was altogether false; for to my Knowledge, being in *England* during some Part of her Majesty's Reign, she did Govern by a Chief Minister; nay, even by two successively; the first whereof was the Lord of *Gedolphin,* and the second the Lord of *Oxford;* so that you have made me *say the thing that was not.* Likewise, in the Account of the Academy of Projectors, and several Passages of my Discourse to my Master *Houyhnhnm,* you have either omitted some material Circumstances, or minced or changed them in such a Manner, that I do hardly know mine own Work. When I formerly hinted to you something of this in a Letter, you were pleased to answer, that you were afraid of giving Offence; that People in Power were very watchful over the Press; and apt not only to interpret, but to punish every thing which looked like an *Inuendo* (as I think you called it.) But pray, how could that which I spoke so many Years ago, and at above five Thousand Leagues distance, in another Reign, be applyed to any of the *Yahoos,* who now are said to govern the Herd; especially, at a time when I little thought on or feared the Unhappiness of living under them: Have not I the most Reason to complain, when I see these very *Yahoos* carried by *Houyhnhnms* in a Vehicle, as if these were Brutes, and those the rational Creatures? And, indeed, to avoid so monstrous and detestable a Sight, was one principal Motive of my Retirement hither.

Thus much I thought proper to tell you in Relation to your self, and to the Trust I reposed in you.

I do in the next Place complain of my own great Want of Judgment, in being prevailed upon by the Intreaties and false Reasonings of you and some others, very much against mine own Opinion, to suffer my Travels to be published. Pray bring to your Mind, how often I desired you to consider, when you insisted on the Motive of *publick Good;* that the *Yahoos* were a Species of Animals utterly incapable of Amendment by Precepts or Examples: And so it hath proved; for instead of seeing a full Stop put to all Abuses and Corruptions, at least in this little Island, as I had Reason to expect: Behold, after above six Months Warning, I cannot learn that my Book hath produced one single Effect according to mine Intentions: I desired you would let me know by a Letter, when Party and Faction were extinguished; Judges learned and upright; Pleaders honest and modest, with some Tincture of common Sense; and *Smithfield* blazing with Pyramids of Law-Books; the young Nobility's Education entirely changed; the Physicians banished; the Female *Yahoos* abounding in Virtue, Honour, Truth and good Sense: Courts and Levees of great Ministers thoroughly weeded and swept; Wit, Merit and Learning rewarded; all Disgracers of the Press in Prose and Verse, condemned to eat nothing but their own Cotten, and quench their Thirst with their own Ink. These, and a Thousand other Reformations, I firmly counted upon by your Encouragement; as indeed they were plainly deducible from the Precepts delivered in my Book. And, it must be owned, that seven Months were a sufficient Time to correct every Vice and Folly to which *Yahoos* are subject; if their Natures had been capable of the least Disposition to Virtue or Wisdom: Yet so far have you been from answering mine Expectation in any of your Letters; that on the contrary, you are loading our Carrier every Week with Libels, and Keys, and Reflections, and Memoirs, and Second Parts; wherein I see myself accused of reflecting upon great States Folk; of degrading human Nature, (for so they have still the Confidence to stile it) and of abusing the Female Sex. I find likewise, that the Writings of those Bundles are not agreed among themselves; for some of them will not allow me to be Author of mine own Travels; and others make me Author of Books to which I am wholly a Stranger.

I find likewise, that your Printer hath been so careless as to confound the Times, and mistake the Dates of my several

Voyages and Returns; neither assigning the true Year, or the true Month, or Day of the Month: And I hear the original Manuscript is all destroyed, since the Publication of my Book. Neither have I any Copy left; however, I have sent you some Corrections, which you may insert, if ever there should be a second Edition: And yet I cannot stand to them, but shall leave that Matter to my judicious and candid Readers, to adjust it as they please.

I hear some of our Sea-*Yahoos* find Fault with my Sea-Language, as not proper in many Parts, nor now in Use. I cannot help it. In my first Voyages, while I was young, I was instructed by the oldest Mariners, and learned to speak as they did. But I have since found that the Sea-*Yahoos* are apt, like the Land ones, to become new fangled in their Words; which the latter change every Year; insomuch, as I remember upon each Return to mine own Country, their old Dialect was so altered, that I could hardly understand the new. And I observe, when any *Yahoo* comes from *London* out of Curiosity to visit me at mine own House, we neither of us are able to deliver our Conceptions in a Manner intelligible to the other.

If the Censure of *Yahoos* could any way affect me, I should have great Reason to complain, that some of them are so bold as to think my Book of Travels a meer Fiction out of mine own Brain; and have gone so far as to drop Hints, that the *Houyhnhnms*, and *Yahoos* have no more Existence than the Inhabitants of *Utopia*.

Indeed I must confess, that as to the People of *Lilliput*, *Brobdingrag*, (for so the Word shall have been spelt, and not erroneously *Brobdingnag*) and *Laputa*; I have never yet heard of any *Yahoo* so presumptuous as to dispute their Being, or the Facts I have related concerning them; because the Truth immediately strikes every Reader with Conviction. And, is there less Probability in my Account of the *Houyhnhnms* or *Yahoos*, when it is manifest as to the latter, there are so many Thousands even in this City, who only differ from their Brother Brutes in *Houyhnhnmland*, because they use a Sort of a *Jabber*, and do not go naked. I wrote for their Amendment, and not their Approbation. The united Praise of the whole Race would be of less Consequence to me, that the neighing of those two degenerate *Houyhnhnms* I keep in my Stable; because, from these, degenerate as they are, I still improve in some Virtues, without any Mixture of Vice.

Do these miserable Animals presume to think that I am so far degenerated as to defend my Veracity; *Yahoo* as I am, it is well known through all *Houyhnhnmland,* that by the Instructions and Examples of my illustrious Master, I was able in the Compass of two Years (although I confess with the utmost Difficulty) to remove that infernal Habit of Lying, Shuffling, Deceiving, and Equivocating, so deeply rooted in the very Souls of all my Species; especially the *Europeans.*

I have other Complaints to make upon this vexatious Occasion; but I forbear troubling myself or you any further. I must freely confess, that since my last Return, some Corruptions of my *Yahoo* Nature have revived in me by conversing with a few of your Species, and particularly those of mine own Family, by an unavoidable Necessity; else I should never have attempted so absurd a Project as that of reforming the *Yahoo* Race in this Kingdom; but, I have now done with all such visionary Schemes for ever.

April 2, 1727

Jonathan Swift's *Gulliver's Travels* is the story of Lemuel Gulliver, a story which ends with the hero's taking up residence with his horses but *begins* with his writing a letter. Although scholars have established that the letter from Gulliver to Sympson was written after the work's first publication and was in fact a kind of advertisement for the new and authoritative Faulkner edition (1735), it matters little, if at all, whether one thinks of the letter as a postscript to the original composition or a preface to the version Swift himself finally approved, since the letter is cast in a fictional mode and, insofar as it represents Gulliver, it maintains a characterization consistent with the one developed in the body of the travels. We stress this point here because a major obstacle to understanding *Gulliver's Travels* has been an unfortunate confusion of Gulliver with his creator. The failure to see that Gulliver is a fictional character, not to be confused with the actual author, Jonathan Swift, makes it difficult to understand the precise uses to which Swift puts Gulliver in the construction of the satire. The letters, at the work's beginning, if analyzed, give us our first understanding of Gulliver's dual function as both the object and the means of the satire and prepare us for what is to follow.

These letters do not make much sense, taken by themselves, for they seem only to voice some very puzzling doubts about the nature of Gulliver-the-author and his intentions in writing his book, not to mention doubt about what in the world is meant by *Yahoos* and *Houyhnhnms* and other seemingly nonsensical terms. However, one impression stands out in the reader's mind above all others: that the author, Gulliver, is annoyed with the way his book has been handled and with the results of its publication. We perceive that he thinks his honesty is in doubt, that his voyage is considered by many to be a hoax, and above all, that his annoyance is not limited to his publisher but extends to the entire human race. He is a recluse who says he prefers the company of his stable horses to that of human beings (or Yahoos, as he mysteriously calls them). We immediately suspect his sanity and his intelligence, for Swift's art has already begun to work, and we are tantalized by the promise of something extraordinary to be revealed. Some attention, therefore, should be paid to a few items in these letters which refer directly to the purpose of Swift's book and to the nature of its satire.

At the time of the book's publication the New World was still a source of mystery and romance to the colonizing European. After the discovery of America and the first exploratory voyages, a kind of literature developed and flourished which was widely popular—the so-called travel literature of men who, actually or not, went on exploratory voyages and came home to report them. These books very soon came into disrepute among reasonable men, whose credulity was strained by accounts of strange monsters and societies and physical wonders that in truth did not exist. It seemed that anyone who so desired could write a book about his supposed voyages and report all kinds of curiosities which were received readily by the gullible public. Gulliver, then, is understandably sensitive to the charge that his book is one of these fakes and that he is an imposter:

> If the Censure of *Yahoos* could any way affect me, I should have great Reason to complain, that some of them are so bold as to think my Book of Travels a meer Fiction

> out of mine own Brain; and have gone so far as to drop
> Hints, that the *Houyhnhnms,* and *Yahoos* have no more Exist-
> ence than the Inhabitants of *Utopia.*

In one sense, then, Swift is writing a parody of the fraudulent
travel literature that flourished in his day, in something of the
same way that Cervantes began *Don Quixote* as a satire of the
chivalric romance which found a wide reception earlier in Eu-
rope. But he is doing more than this, and the question of Gulliver's honesty within the fictional world Swift creates for him
will ultimately be included in the larger question of the de-
pendability of his insights and their relevance to the real world.

Nevertheless, it is important to Swift's purpose to define
for us the particular kind of honesty Gulliver has, and the quar-
rel between Gulliver and Sympson over the disposition of the
manuscript is thus extremely important. In his answer to Gulliver's charge that he has not followed his specific instructions,
Sympson manages, with a delicacy perhaps born of long dealing
with cranky authors, to vindicate himself without disqualifying
Gulliver's account of his travels or making him out to be a liar:

> Before he (Gulliver) quitted *Redriff,* he left the Custody of
> the following Papers in my Hands, with the Liberty to dis-
> pose of them as I should think fit. I have carefully perused
> them three Times: The Style is very plain and simple; and
> the only Fault I find is, that the Author, after the manner
> of Travellers, is a little too circumstantial. There is an air
> of Truth apparent through the whole; and indeed the
> Author was so distinguished for his Veracity, that it be-
> came a Sort of Proverb among his Neighbours at *Redriff,*
> when any one affirmed a Think, to say, it was as true as
> if Mr. Gulliver had spoke it.

Gulliver, says Sympson, is a "little too circumstantial," a seemingly slight fault, but one upon which a great deal of the satire
depends. For Gulliver *is* circumstantial, as one may see from
the way he reports what he saw and what he felt. His observations are recorded in the most minute detail and, moreover,
until the very end, without much emotion. He is so careful of
every detail that, ignoring for the moment the special nature

of his report, we are free to read it without any more doubt about its truth than the truth of an algebra textbook. This deadpan style, typical of detached, factual reporting, accounts for much of the humor. For how can one remain "objective" while relating, say, the grotesque and humorous manner in which the fire in the Queen's palace is extinguished (Book I)? In short, the discrepancy between the style of narration (objective, detached, scientific) and the subject of the narrative (fantastic) is one of the primary sources of the satire's success. Even as we are taken in by the sheer force of the details of his narration and the new perspective they press upon us, we are at the same time compelled to keep the literal-minded Gulliver constantly before us. The question is thus posed: *Even if he is not lying, what is the value of Gulliver's "truth"?* For what is important is the degree of truth in Gulliver's reasoning, the validity of those conclusions at which he arrives, whether or not he actually saw what he claims to have seen.

Note, for example, in the letter from Gulliver, the long tirade against those who have read the travels and yet not profited thereby:

> Behold, after above six Months Warning, I cannot learn that my Book hath produced one single Effect according to mine Intentions: I desired you [Sympson] would let me know by a Letter, when Party and Faction were extinguished; Judges learned and upright; Pleaders honest and modest . . . the Physicians banished; the Female *Yahoos* abounding in Virtue, Honour, Truth and good Sense . . . Wit, Merit and Learning rewarded. . . . These, and a Thousand other Reformations, I firmly counted upon by your Encouragement; as indeed they were plainly deducible from the Precepts delivered in my Book. And, it must be owned, that seven months were a sufficient Time to correct every Vice and Folly to which *Yahoos* are subject; if their Natures had been capable of the least Disposition to Virtue or Wisdom.

Here, in a letter written after the journeys, after the experience of Gulliver's encounters with foreign populations and personages, we do have emotion; we have, moreover, spleen, or misanthropy, for this is what the journeys lead to in Gulliver's case: a complete rejection of humankind. But we have something else. We have the quality in Gulliver that probably gives him his name—gullibility, or, perhaps, naïveté. Here is the naïveté of a man who thinks seven months is enough time for a nation to see the error of its vanity and to become virtuous and sensible. The question is again posed, even before we read the travels: What has Gulliver learned, and how has he reacted to it? How far can we trust him to see an important truth, and how far can we follow *his* lead in our own emotional, moral, and intellectual response to what we see through his eyes?

As we have shown, much of the satire in *Gulliver's Travels* is directed against Gulliver and what he stands for. And yet, it is Gulliver's discourse which must carry the attack against the rest of humankind. As it turns out, he says much in his disapproval of human folly with which Swift plainly agrees. To achieve this occasional fusion of sentiment without destroying the humorous characterization of Gulliver already established, the real author, Swift, endows the fictional author-narrator, Gulliver, with a style of expression that becomes increasingly ironic as Gulliver becomes increasingly disenchanted with his species. Take for example the word *Inuendo* which we find in the letter to Sympson:

> . . . you were pleased to answer [Gulliver's charges that his text had been tampered with], that you were afraid of giving offence; that People in Power were very watchful over the Press; and apt not only to interpret, but to punish every thing which looked like an *Inuendo* (as I think you called it.)

As Gulliver uses the word—a form of the Latin *innuere*, "to give a nod," which meant in Swift's time, as it does now, a deprecatory insinuation—the word is misspelled and italicized. The use of italics conforms with eighteenth-century convention in that the practice of underlining was somewhat indiscriminate. Spelling, too, was not as uniform as it is today. Nevertheless, *innuendo* spelled as we spell it and meaning what we mean by it seems first to have appeared in 1678. It is not therefore likely that Swift was ignorant of what he was doing when he has Gulli-

ver misspell the word (unless this is a compositor's error), especially since Gulliver uses the word in a very self-conscious way,
as if it were rather unclean and as if he desired, as soon as possible, to wipe it from his pen. Gulliver is either unfamiliar with
the word or wishes to appear so. Moreover he cannot, or pretends not (it makes little difference for characterization), to
remember whether, indeed, this was the word Sympson used.
Finally, he appears to detest the word; first, for its meaning,
suggesting as it does a duplicity in man which he would be the
last in the world to confess in himself, especially in the matter
of his profession as author; and, second, because the word is
faintly effete, faintly pretentious—that curious kind of word
which always sounds, however legitimate it may in fact be,
snobbish, exotic, special, and, therefore, unnecessary. This is
how it must appear to the outraged Gulliver who later in the
letter writes:

> I hear some of our Sea-*Yahoos* find Fault with my Sea-
> Language, as not proper in many Parts, nor now in Use.
> I cannot help it. . . . I was instructed by the oldest Mari-
> ners, and learned to speak as they did. But I have since
> found that the Sea-*Yahoos* are apt, like the Land ones, to
> become new-fangled in their Words; . . . And I observe,
> when any *Yahoo* comes from *London* out of Curiosity to
> visit me at mine own House, we neither of us are able to de-
> liver our Conceptions in a Manner intelligible to the other.

Nevertheless, Gulliver, mad as he is, is here Swift's persona,
doing Swift's work, putting forth the author's viewpoint. It is
Swift who is conscious that language is a moral instrument and
it is Swift who would, moreover, purge from human affairs that
meanness which necessitates a word like *innuendo*. The evidence
for this is abundant in all of Swift's writing and nowhere more
concisely represented than in the later episodes in *Gulliver's
Travels*. These later episodes, as do those of all works which are
units rather than aggregates, begin, in fact, at the beginning of
the work.

We have, on the one hand, a report of a journey written
in a straightforward, matter-of-fact style, calculated to get the
trust of the reader. On the other hand, we are warned by this

letter, even before we read about the journey, that we are deal-ing with a crank, a misanthropist, who may or may not be worth listening to. In any event, Swift is taking care at the beginning to see that *he* is not confused with his creation, with his char-acter. Gulliver is not Swift, and this is very important, for read-ers are inclined to suppose that Swift is the misanthropist, not Gulliver. They are offended by the scatology and say Swift has a dirty mind (not Gulliver, who until the very end reveals no more emotion about fecal matter than he does about his own country's use of gunpowder). They are offended at the analogy drawn between Yahoos and human beings and fail to see that it is Gulliver, not Swift, who calls his kind Yahoos.

The point is that Swift takes such pains to make the reader see Gulliver as a separate entity that it is surprising he can still be confused with his creator. *Swift does not allow us for a minute to stop looking at Gulliver from a distance:* we are constantly being put off by Gulliver's essential obtuseness and lack of imagina-tion. The first pages of his narration of his journey to Lilliput are practically enough to establish in our minds the kind of prideful character he is at the beginning of his journey and to make understandable his final rejection of mankind once he has been stripped of this false pride only to substitute another.

Gulliver sees a great deal, and as we follow him through his journeys, seeing what he sees, we learn a great deal. But though we are looking at the same phenomena, Gulliver learns one thing, and we learn another. His point of view is not our point of view. On the second if not the first reading, the letters lead the way into the work's meaning.

FROM GHOSTS **ACT ONE**

SCENE: *A large room looking upon a garden. A door in the left-hand wall, and two in the right. In the middle of the room, a round table with chairs set about it, and books, magazines, and newspapers upon it. In the foreground on the left, a window, by which is a small sofa with a work-table in front of it. At the back the room opens into a conservatory rather smaller than the room. From the right-hand side of this a door leads to the garden. Through the large panes of glass that form the outer wall of the conservatory, a gloomy fjord landscape can be discerned, half ob-scured by a steady rain.*

ENGSTRAND *is standing close up to the garden door. His left leg is slightly deformed, and he wears a boot with a clump of wood under the sole.* REGINA, *with an empty garden-syringe in her hand, is trying to prevent his coming in.*

REGINA *(below her breath).*   What is it you want? Stay where you are. The rain is dripping off you.

ENGSTRAND.   God's good rain, my girl.

REGINA.   The Devil's own rain, that's what it is!

ENGSTRAND.   Lord, how you talk, Regina. *(Takes a few limping steps forward.)* What I wanted to tell you was this——

REGINA.   Don't clump around like that, stupid! The young master is lying asleep upstairs.

ENGSTRAND.   Asleep still? In the middle of the day?

REGINA.   Well, it's no business of yours.

ENGSTRAND.   I was out on the spree last night——

REGINA.   I don't doubt it.

ENGSTRAND.   Yes, we are poor weak mortals, my girl——

REGINA.   We are indeed.

ENGSTRAND.   — and the temptations of the world are manifold, you know—but, for all that, here I was at my work at half-past five this morning.

REGINA.   Yes, yes, but make yourself scarce now. I am not going to stand here as if I had a rendezvous with you.

ENGSTRAND.   As if you had a what?

REGINA.   I am not going to have any one find you here: so now you know, and you can go.

ENGSTRAND *(coming a few steps nearer).*   Not a bit of it! Not before we have had a little chat. This afternoon I shall have finished my job down at the school house, and I shall be off home to town by to-night's boat.

REGINA *(mutters).*   Pleasant journey to you!

ENGSTRAND.   Thanks, my girl. To-morrow is the opening of the Orphanage, and I expect there will be a fine kick-up here and plenty of good strong drink, don't you know. And no one shall say of Jacob Engstrand that he can't hold off when temptation comes in his way.

REGINA.   Oho!

ENGSTRAND.   Yes, because there will be a lot of fine folk here to-morrow. Parson Manders is expected from town, too.

REGINA.   What is more, he's coming to-day.

ENGSTRAND.   There you are! And I'm going to be precious careful he doesn't have anything to say against me,-do you see?

REGINA.   Oh, that's your game, is it?

ENGSTRAND.   What do you mean?

REGINA *(with a significant look at him)*.   What is it you want to
humbug Mr. Manders out of, this time?

ENGSTRAND.   Sh! Sh! Are you crazy? Do you suppose *I* would
want to humbug Mr. Manders? No, no —. Mr. Manders
has always been too kind a friend for me to do that. But
what I wanted to talk to you about, was my going back
home to-night.

REGINA.   The sooner you go, the better I shall be pleased.

ENGSTRAND.   Yes, only I want to take you with me, Regina.

REGINA *(open-mouthed)*.   You want to take me——? What did
you say?

ENGSTRAND.   I want to take you home with me, I said.

REGINA *(contemptuously)*.   You will never get me home with you.

ENGSTRAND.   Ah, we shall see about that.

REGINA.   Yes, you can be quite certain we *shall* see about that.
I, who have been brought up by a lady like Mrs. Alving?
— I, who have been treated almost as if I were her own
child? — do you suppose I am going home with *you*? — to
such a house as yours? Not likely!

ENGSTRAND.   What the devil do you mean? Are you setting
yourself up against your father, you hussy?

REGINA *(mutters, without looking at him)*.   You have often told me
I was none of yours.

ENGSTRAND.   Bah! — why do you want to pay any attention to
that?

REGINA.   Haven't you many and many a time abused me and
called me a——? *Fi donc!*

ENGSTRAND.   I'll swear I never used such an ugly word.

REGINA.   Oh, it doesn't matter what word you used.

ENGSTRAND.   Besides, that was only when I was a bit fuddled
— hm! Temptations are manifold in this world, Regina.

REGINA.   Ugh!

ENGSTRAND.   And it was when your mother was in a nasty
temper. I had to find some way of getting my knife into

her, my girl. She was always so precious genteel. *(Mimicking her.)* "Let go, Jacob! Let me be! Please to remember that I was three years with the Alvings at Rosenvold, and they were people who went to Court!" *(Laughs.)* Bless my soul, she never could forget that Captain Alving got a Court appointment while she was in service here.

REGINA.   Poor mother — you worried her into her grave pretty soon.

ENGSTRAND *(shrugging his shoulders)*.   Of course, of course; I have got to take the blame for everything.

REGINA *(beneath her breath, as she turns away)*.   Ugh — that leg, too!

ENGSTRAND.   What are you saying, my girl?

REGINA.   *Pied de mouton.*

ENGSTRAND.   Is that English?

REGINA.   Yes.

ENGSTRAND.   You have had a good education out here, and no mistake; and it may stand you in good stead now, Regina.

REGINA *(after a short silence)*.   And what was it you wanted me to come to town for?

ENGSTRAND.   Need you ask why a father wants his only child? Ain't I a poor lonely widower?

REGINA.   Oh, don't come to me with that tale. Why do you want me to go?

ENGSTRAND.   Well, I must tell you I am thinking of taking up a new line now.

REGINA *(whistles)*.   You have tried that so often — but it has always proved a fool's errand.

ENGSTRAND.   Ah, but this time you will just see, Regina! Strike me dead if——

REGINA *(stamping her feet)*.   Stop swearing!

ENGSTRAND.   Sh! Sh! — you're quite right, my girl, quite right! What I wanted to say was only this, that I have put by a tidy penny out of what I have made by working at this new Orphanage up here.

REGINA.   Have you? All the better for you.

ENGSTRAND.   What is there for a man to spend his money on, out here in the country?

REGINA.   Well, what then?

ENGSTRAND. Well, you see, I thought of putting the money into something that would pay. I thought of some kind of an eating-house for seafaring folk——

REGINA. HEAVENS!

ENGSTRAND. Oh, a high-class eating-house, of course,—not a pigsty for common sailors. Damn it, no; it would be a place ships' captains and first mates would come to; really good sort of people, you know.

REGINA. And what should I——?

ENGSTRAND. You would help there. But only to make a show, you know. You wouldn't find it hard work, I can promise you, my girl. You should do exactly as you liked.

REGINA. Oh, yes, quite so!

ENGSTRAND. But we must have some women in the house; that is as clear as daylight. Because in the evening we must make the place a little attractive — some singing and dancing, and that sort of thing. Remember they are seafolk — wayfarers on the waters of life! *(Coming nearer to her.)* Now don't be a fool and stand in your own way, Regina. What good are you going to do here? Will this education, that your mistress has paid for, be of any use? You are to look after the children in the new Home, I hear. Is that the sort of work for you? Are you so frightfully anxious to go and wear out your health and strength for the sake of these dirty brats?

REGINA. No, if things were to go as I want them to, then——. Well, it may happen; who knows? It may happen!

ENGSTRAND. What may happen?

REGINA. Never you mind. Is it much that you have put by, up here?

ENGSTRAND. Taking it all round, I should say about forty or fifty pounds.

REGINA. That's not so bad.

ENGSTRAND. It's enough to make a start with, my girl.

REGINA. Don't you mean to give me any of the money?

ENGSTRAND. No, I'm hanged if I do.

REGINA. Don't you mean to send me as much as a dress-length of stuff, just for once?

ENGSTRAND. Come and live in the town with me and you shall have plenty of dresses.

REGINA.   Pooh! — I can get that much for myself, if I have
a mind to.

ENGSTRAND.   But it's far better to have a father's guiding hand,
Regina. Just now I can get a nice house in Little Harbour
Street. They don't want much money down for it — and
we could make it like a sort of seamen's home, don't you
know.

REGINA.   But I have no intention of living with you! I have
nothing whatever to do with you. So now, be off!

ENGSTRAND.   You wouldn't be living with me long, my girl.
No such luck — not if you knew how to play your cards.
Such a fine wench as you have grown this last year or
two——

REGINA.   Well——?

ENGSTRAND.   It wouldn't be very long before some first mate
came along—or perhaps a captain.

REGINA.   I don't mean to marry a man of that sort. Sailors
have no *savoir-vivre.*

ENGSTRAND.   What haven't they got?

REGINA.   I know what sailors are, I tell you. They aren't the
sort of people to marry.

ENGSTRAND.   Well, don't bother about marrying them. You can
make it pay just as well. *(More confidentially.)* That fellow —
the Englishman — the one with the yacht — he gave
seventy pounds, he did; and she wasn't a bit prettier than
you.

REGINA *(advancing towards him).*   Get out!

ENGSTRAND *(stepping back).*   Here! here! — you're not going to
hit me, I suppose?

REGINA.   Yes! If you talk like that of mother, I *will* hit you.
Get out, I tell you! *(Pushes him up to the garden door.)* And
don't bang the doors. Young Mr. Alving——

ENGSTRAND.   Is asleep—I know. It's funny how anxious you
are about young Mr. Alving. *(In a lower tone.)* Oho! is it
possible that it is *he* that——?

REGINA.   Get out, and be quick about it! Your wits are wan-
dering, my good man. No, don't go that way; Mr. Manders
is just coming along. Be off down the kitchen stairs.

ENGSTRAND *(moving towards the right).*   Yes, yes — all right. But
have a bit of a chat with him that's coming along. He's

the chap to tell you what a child owes to its father. For I am your father, anyway, you know. I can prove it by the Register.

This is the opening scene of *Ghosts* by Henrik Ibsen, one of the first classics of realistic drama. The setting is described in some detail, and we may visualize the stage as the curtain rises on Act One. It is an ordinary interior, but the gloomy landscape outside the windows dominates the atmosphere, and the rain suggests the emotional "weather" of the play.

The dialogue is between two menials—a thoroughly conventional way to begin and one that might be considered a dramatic cliché. It makes sense for the playwright not to introduce his most important characters until he has informed his audience of the play's circumstances and has aroused their interest. Hence the conversation between a maid and a butler or between a housekeeper and a delivery boy is a familiar device. They can gossip about the people of the house in a natural enough way, and in the process we begin to learn what we must know about the chief characters. This initial exchange between Regina and Engstrand performs such a function in *Ghosts,* a function referred to by the term *dramatic exposition.* The scene provides us with considerable information, some of it important in ways we must wait to discover. There is a "young master" —presumably a son—in the household. His late sleeping draws comment. Are his habits out of the ordinary? Is something the matter with him? A new orphanage is being opened, and the mistress of the house has some connection with it. The expected visit of a Parson Manders is considered to be of importance; Regina suspects Engstrand wants to use him in some way. No sooner do we learn that Engstrand is Regina's father than doubt concerning his paternity is introduced. Engstrand plans to open a hangout for sailors and wants Regina to help in the business as a kind of hostess. But Regina, who has grown up in Mrs. Alving's home, scorns both that idea and the prospect of managing children in the orphanage. In her affected gentility she seems to take after her dead mother, who also served in the Alving household and who was involved improperly with an English yachtsman. Regina's aspirations may, as Engstrand suspects, be fixed upon the son (and when we learn a bit later in the play that young Alving has recently returned from Paris, that throws a certain light on Regina's mannered use of French phrases).

This is quite a bit to pack into a few lines of dialogue, but Ibsen manages it smoothly. Moreover, the content of the scene goes far beyond simple exposition; it is rich in characterization and foreshadowing, it introduces themes and establishes attitudes that dominate the action, and it initiates a series of relationships between these lesser characters and the three major ones that form an important part of the play.

Regina's first words to Engstrand startle us by their harsh resentment; to keep a lame old man standing in the rain is an almost definitive act of uncharity. They talk about the weather, but to notice this is to realize how the playwright has, in this case too, transformed a cliché by making it the means of achieving subtler dramatic purposes. This opening exchange underscores the pervasive atmosphere, but more than that it sets forth a significant antithesis. "God's good rain, my girl," says Engstrand, mild and conciliatory. "The devil's own rain," Regina retorts, and the clash of character—or the tension between attitudes—which is the essence of Ibsen's plays, is clear. Just after this scene with Engstrand, Regina will answer Pastor Manders' casual grumbling about the weather by saying, "It's a splendid rain for the farmers, Mr. Manders." The bitter rejoinder to Engstrand will have enabled us to gauge such "thoughtful" words to Manders and to understand that she is playing upon the gullible pastor for her own purposes. Thus even that hoary topic of small talk, the weather, provides a telling means of characterization. The same is true of Engstrand's remark. His piety about God's rain is followed by an admission that he was carousing the night before. It is not the fact of his carousal that is so damaging as the style of the confession, framed in platitudes about mortal weakness and worldly temptation. Even though Engstrand speaks mockingly of his dead wife and calls orphans "brats," his hypocrisy is of a subtler sort than Regina's. His frailties, both physical and moral, deserve pity; but he parades these as if they were marks of honor. His lameness can be seen as the emblem of this quality in Engstrand, and if it recalls to us Satan's traditional deformity of the cloven foot (Regina calls him "sheep-foot"), the sign carries particularly ironic overtones. Although Engstrand cuts a pathetic figure, rain-soaked and full of pious phrases, the rain is identified as "the devil's own," and we know how apt the devil is at quoting Scripture.

Already these menials are commanding the attention due fully delineated characters, but we can see too that characterization is conveyed by means that also lead us to expect specific themes. Though their purposes and attitudes clash, Engstrand and Regina both betray a disparity between actual and assumed character that we justifiably call hypocrisy. Indeed, pretense—especially as it takes the form of excessive concern with appearances—is a dominant note. Regina does not wish to be seen having a rendezvous with Engstrand; he, on the other hand, is "going to be precious careful he [Pastor Manders] doesn't have anything to say against me." Each expresses shocked disapproval of the rough language the other uses. Thus in these initial depictions of a drunken carpenter who mouths moral sentiments and a hard-hearted young servant girl with pretentions to refinement, the play focuses our attention upon human dissimulation. We are confronted, from the beginning, with the contradiction between social appearances and private realities.

If we examine this beginning scene with a view to its dramatic effect, we must certainly note a line of emphasis that has not yet been mentioned. For the fact that Engstrand and Regina are—ostensibly at least—father and daughter is not simply revealed casually in the course of the exposition; it is calculated to come upon us with a real measure of shock. As we have observed, Regina's initial behavior toward Engstrand would be harsh treatment to any old man. She acts as if Engstrand is nothing more to her than a tiresome and overly familiar acquaintance. When he says he wants Regina to come home with him, we perhaps interpret her indignation as merely the response due an outrageous proposal. Thereupon we learn the man is her father, but we find almost at the same time that he has denied it. Then, as if matters between this father and daughter were not disquieting enough, we hear Engstrand's shady offer to employ Regina as a "hostess" at his "seamen's home." He speaks of "a father's guiding hand," but he reminds his daughter that there are other profitable arrangements she might make with a man besides marriage. Surely the first glimpse this play gives of the parent-child relation is hardly an ideal one, and the more we understand of it the worse it appears. Moreover, other aspects of family life are equally dark. Engstrand bitterly recalls his wife's coldness to him, and yet her affair with the English yachtsman puts his wife's supposed "gentility" in ironic perspective. Regina, for her part, sees marriage as a challenge to make the best deal possible.

The implications of Ibsen's opening scene are immensely suggestive. What is involved is not merely the delineation of two secondary characters, but indeed the establishment of the dark atmosphere of the play's main action. For here is a world where fathers can be left standing in the rain by their children, where daughters may be urged by their fathers to sell themselves, where husbands recall their dead wives' lovers, where orphans are referred to as "dirty brats," and where not even a wise child knows her own father.

And such possibilities are presented not in a context that is overtly sordid or cynical but, on the contrary, in one of apparent respectability. In fact, there is an emphasis on appearances —on the conventional look of things—that gives these moral distortions their particular point. In the sphere of actual relationships Regina shows no respect at all for her living parent, but when the abstract matter of her mother's honor comes up, her reactions are conventionally and vigorously respectable. Similarly, Engstrand can urge Regina to most indecent courses, yet in doing so employ the moral commonplace about "what a child owes to its father." Thus we may conclude that one of the crucial functions of this play's opening scene is to show conventional attitudes and ideals as concealments or evasions of the truth and to suggest family relationships as the particular realm of such deceptions. The play will shift its focus to other characters, but the beginning has, in the manner of an overture, announced the principal themes.

At the end of the passage we have reprinted, Regina drives Engstrand off, turning a deaf ear to his schemes. But he indicates that she has not heard the last of the matter. "For I am your father, anyway, you know," he says, "I can prove it by the Register." Here is the crowning touch to the thematic hints the scene has given; we confront the issue of social appearances versus private realities in its epitome. The Register, an official

document, exemplifies all that is legitimate and socially sanc-
tioned, but it is a legitimacy that does not express reality but
rather suppresses it. Whatever the truth of Engstrand's relation
to Regina, whether conceived in terms of biological or psychological parenthood, the "proof" of the Register is invoked as
an overriding authority. Both the literal reality of blood relationship and the figurative, but equally valid, reality of the heart's
acceptance or rejection are thus ignored. Engstrand himself
may not sense the irony in this; his words reflect the assumption, which reverberates through the entire scene, that society
defines truth only by its own conventional fictions.

How the play will go on to develop this theme we do not
yet know at this early point in the action. But the dramatist has
already suggested something of the subsequent pattern. The
contrasting expressions on the weather—at the very beginning
—are, as we saw, a deft piece of characterization, but they are
also the presentation of a basic conflict of views that goes beyond
its relevance to character.

> ENGSTRAND.   God's good rain, my girl.
> REGINA.   The devil's own rain, that's what it is!

Engstrand's is the voice of bland and pious acceptance; Regina's,
for the moment, is that of spirited, persistent realism. And in
that moment she speaks not only for herself but perhaps for
Ibsen as well. At least what he gives us here in miniature is that
rejection and unmasking of platitude, that confrontation of shallow illusion by stark reality, which is to characterize the later
action of the play.

Chapter Seven   **D**   *Interpretation and Evaluation*

espite a common concern with literature, the interpretations and judgments of critics differ greatly, not only because of differing temperaments and times, but because of the differing premises on which they base their understanding of literature, and because of the different aspects of literature they choose to emphasize. Yet this diversity of premises does not support the idea of a "whirligig of taste," the idea that all judgments on literature are arbitrary and subjective. Nor does it support the related notion that all criticism is futile. The premises of criticism are intelligible and may be discussed intelligently. In matters of taste there *are* disputes, and out of them can come, if not agreement on critical premises, at least a deeper understanding of individual works.

PREMISES FOR UNDERSTANDING LITERATURE

The major premises on which critics base their efforts to understand literature may be stated as five propositions.[1] These propositions are that literature may be understood as:

1. a kind of *knowledge* of men and events;
2. a *criticism* of men and events;
3. an *effect* of which men and events are causes;
4. a *cause* of certain effects in men and events;

1 An excellent description of critical premises is to be found in Chapter I of M. H. Abrams, *The Mirror and the Lamp* (New York: Oxford University Press, 1953).

5. an *esthetic object,* that is, a unique construct of the imagination.

These propositions are exhaustive but not exclusive. In good criticism one proposition is rarely found without traces of the others. In fact, the best criticism of literature is marked by a conscious recognition of the value of the alternatives to it. This is not merely the canny hedging of the oracle. It follows from the complexity of literature itself, which, like all complex experience, evokes multiple interpretation. That a work leads men to approach it in various ways is often a sign of its excellence. In any case, a perfect agreement of critics would be possible only about nonsense, and not about the most interesting sort of nonsense either.

In spite of the arguments of critics, the propositions underlying their views often seem more complementary than contradictory; and all promise applications that are somewhat, if not equally, fruitful. A *criticism* of life implies, after all, some *knowledge,* however limited, of men and events. Certainly literature may help enlarge our *knowledge* if we explore its *cause* and *effect* relations with its author and audience and with their times. Almost inevitably we conduct such an exploration when we try to identify references and allusions. But none of these explorations logically excludes examination of the formal structures which make literary works *esthetic objects.*

For example, Shelley's "Ode to the West Wind" is a criticism or evaluation of life in the sense that it attaches value— at times overtly, at times by implication—to some kinds of human behavior, while neglecting or rejecting others. By the very fact of its existence the poem is a way of valuing human expression, and by its form a way of valuing art. These, together with the tribute of great care in its descriptive images, are ways of valuing both nature and human sensitivity. In fact, all five premises may be applied to a consideration of Shelley's poem.

ODE TO THE WEST WIND

I.

O wild West Wind, thou breath of Autumn's being,
Thou, from whose unseen presence the leaves dead
Are driven, like ghosts from an enchanter fleeing,

Yellow, and black, and pale, and hectic red,
Pestilence-stricken multitudes: O thou,
Who chariotest to their dark wintry bed

The wingéd seeds, where they lie cold and low,
Each like a corpse within its grave, until
Thine azure sister of the Spring shall blow

Her clarion o'er the dreaming earth, and fill
(Driving sweet buds like flocks to feed in air)
With living hues and odours plain and hill:

Wild Spirit, which art moving everywhere;
Destroyer and preserver; hear, oh, hear!

II.

Thou on whose stream, mid the steep sky's commotion,
Loose clouds like earth's decaying leaves are shed,
Shook from the tangled boughs of Heaven and Ocean,

Angels of rain and lightning: there are spread
On the blue surface of thine aëry surge,
Like the bright hair uplifted from the head

Of some fierce Maenad, even from the dim verge
Of the horizon to the zenith's height,
The locks of the approaching storm. Thou dirge

Of the dying year, to which this closing night
Will be the dome of a vast sepulchre,
Vaulted with all thy congregated might

Of vapours, from whose solid atmosphere
Black rain, and fire, and hail will burst: oh hear!

III.

Thou who didst waken from his summer dreams
The blue Mediterranean, where he lay,
Lulled by the coil of his crystalline streams,

Beside a pumice isle in Baiae's bay,
And saw in sleep old palaces and towers
Quivering within the wave's intenser day,

All overgrown with azure moss and flowers
So sweet, the sense faints picturing them! Thou
For whose path the Atlantic's level powers

Cleave themselves into chasms, while far below
The sea-blooms and the oozy woods which wear
The sapless foliage of the ocean, know

Thy voice, and suddenly grow gray with fear,
And tremble and despoil themselves: oh, hear!

IV.

If I were a dead leaf thou mightest bear,
If I were a swift cloud to fly with thee;
A wave to pant beneath thy power, and share

The impulse of thy strength, only less free
Than thou, O uncontrollable! If even
I were as in my boyhood, and could be

The comrade of thy wanderings over Heaven,
As then, when to outstrip thy skiey speed
Scarce seemed a vision; I would ne'er have striven

As thus with thee in prayer in my sore need.
Oh, lift me as a wave, a leaf, a cloud!
I fall upon the thorns of life! I bleed!

A heavy weight of hours has chained, and bowed
One too like thee: tameless, and swift, and proud.

V.

Make me thy lyre, even as the forest is:
What if my leaves are falling like its own!
The tumult of thy mighty harmonies

Will take from both a deep, autumnal tone,
Sweet though in sadness. Be thou, Spirit fierce,
My spirit! Be thou me, impetuous one!

Drive my dead thoughts over the universe
Like withered leaves to quicken a new birth!
And, by the incantation of this verse,

Scatter, as from an unextinguished hearth,
Ashes and sparks, my words among mankind!
Be through my lips to unawakened earth

The trumpet of a prophecy! O, Wind,
If Winter comes, can Spring be far behind?

APPLYING THE PREMISES

The invocation of the West Wind as a *Spirit* which is both *Destroyer* and *Preserver* embodies the poet's apparent beliefs in animism and in the identity of the destructive and creative forces in the universe. These are essential to understanding the view of experience underlying the poem. Even a first reading will uncover other evaluations: a passionate attachment to personal freedom, an optimism about the role of poetry in human affairs and about the rebirth of suppressed human powers. The poem's statement of the inevitability of political change: "If Winter comes can Spring be far behind," is not merely a "political" statement. It suggests that politics is part of a natural cycle. This, in turn, relates politics to myths of death and rebirth and to their religious analogues. In these biological and mythic analogies, however, there is the clear implication that politics is in some sense beyond human control. Perhaps this would explain why Shelley chooses to address Nature in the person of the West Wind rather than to address men. The Ode, then, presents a quite complex criticism of men and events, not only in overt statements, but in implications and even— as was just noted—in such "technical" details as the mode of address.

But beyond this criticism of men and events the poem presents at least two kinds of *knowledge* about them. First, there is the poet's knowledge of the matters the poem deals with. The poem is, in part, an observation of nature and an attempted description of the process of history. Second, there is the knowledge of the poet and his times that others may extract from the poem itself. While the "Ode to the West Wind" is neither a psychological case study nor a historical document in the sense of being a comprehensive record of men and events, it is at least suggestive of how a keen mind reacted at a moment in history and, specifically, of how it reacted to the matters treated in the poem. In these two senses the poem may impart knowledge ranging from the appearance of clouds at a certain season to knowledge of how an English intellectual viewed the historical process in the early nineteenth century.

But if Shelley's "Ode" is a criticism of life and a possible source of knowledge, it is also linked in a chain of *cause* and *effect*. It is an *effect* of Shelley's temperament and talent and is also affected by pressures exerted by his times and by the traditions of poetry. Understanding the poem as effect leads us to consider matters as diverse as the politics of the French Revolution, Shelley's state of mind at the time of the poem's composition, and the history of the ode as a poetic genre. Yet not all these considerations are of equal importance, for all are transmuted by Shelley's imagination as it creates the poem, and it is the poem itself, not *a priori* ideas of what is important, that determines how fruitful or relevant any particular consideration will be.

Understanding the poem as *cause* leads again to a great diversity of concerns. The poem may be the cause of changes in the poet himself, and it may influence other poets in various ways. The "West Wind" ode has certainly been a cause of feeling and reflection, perhaps even of action, in critics and readers. It has, however slightly, modified the course of English verse. Understanding these effects is a valid, though partial, way of understanding the poem. But none of these ways of understanding eliminates the value of attempting to understand the poem as a unity of structures in language, idea, and form—that is, as an *esthetic object*. We may still discuss with profit how the interlocking form of *terza rima* relates to the poem's cyclical view of history, how both are confirmed by the intense, then lapsing, emotional quality created through the diction—and so on until we have examined the significant relations of the parts of the poem. In fact, it is probably necessary to consider the poem as an esthetic object first, in order to confirm that we are reading historical or philosophic notions out of it, rather than reading them into it.

Apparently, all the critical propositions are fruitful in the sense that they suggest specific questions about individual works. But some are too fruitful. Questions about Shelley's knowledge of the topography of Baiae's Bay or about the reception of the "Ode" in Council Bluffs, while arising naturally from the propositions, may contribute nothing to our understanding of the poem. One of Shakespeare's characters says of pedants that "they have been at a great feast of languages and stolen the scraps." A work of literature is such a feast, not a famine in which one must struggle over crumbs. Beyond the compulsion which leads people to save string, there is little justification for the accumulation of random "fact." The essential strategy in understanding literature is first to isolate *relevant* questions.

Unfortunately there is no wholly reliable rule of thumb for determining relevance, since relevance depends on contexts, and each work of literature is unique. But the propositions themselves seem to fall into a rough order of inclusiveness and usefulness. For example, questions arising from the view of literature as *cause* or as *effect* are likely to apply primarily to ideas and less frequently to language and form, although questions arising from the former proposition often do apply to language and form. The view of literature as an *esthetic object*—that is, a unique entity of language, idea, and form—is likely to lead continually to questions relevant to all three.

Questions about the accuracy of Shelley's descriptions (*knowledge*), his view of history (*criticism*), the relation of his poem to the industrialization of England (*effect*), its influence on later poetry (*cause*) sometimes create the danger that they will be pursued as ends in themselves. In addition, they may lead to a distorted view of the poem by forcing us to discuss it simply as a set of ideas rather than as a complex organization of which ideas are one subordinate aspect. For these reasons the proposition that literature is to be understood as an esthetic object seems to be the most useful single proposition, at least for an initial consideration of most works. But the actual writings of critics rarely deal with questions arising from one proposition. The "schools" of criticism derive from combinations of propositions. These combinations are extremely diverse, but it is possible to isolate several important ones.

A critic may choose to deal with questions that are common to several propositions. For example, Kenneth Burke's view that literary form is identical with the psychology of the audience leads him to deal consistently with questions arising from both the propositions that a literary work is to be understood as a *cause* and as an *esthetic object.*

Other kinds of criticism deal with questions which arise from several propositions, but which are at the same time relevant to a discipline outside literature. Three important examples of this are *moral, psychological,* and *historical* criticism. A critic primarily interested in *moral* questions will concern himself with the ethical meanings of the work. This would involve not simply the moral implications of the plot and characters if the work is a novel, but also the responsibility with which the author employs language and form. It would, in addition, explore the work as an ethical response to the author's times and examine the possible ethical effects of the work on its audience. *Psychological criticism* investigates such problems as the work's relation to the psychological make-up of its author, the view of human behavior the work suggests, and the psychological aspects of its effects on its audience, not only through its ideas but through its language and form as well. *Historical criticism* (which in some variants is called *sociological criticism*) attempts to view the work both as a cause and an effect of historical circumstances. This involves not merely a concern with the political consequences of the work but, in the writing of critics concerned with the "history of ideas," with its intellectual antecedents and effects. A special type of historical criticism concentrates on the relation of a literary work to the traditions of literature itself.

Two outstanding kinds of recent criticism deal with questions based on many premises but having a common relevance to a specific body of belief. These are *Marxist* and *Freudian* criticism. They may be thought of as types of historical and psychological criticism, but in them there is an overt commitment to a specific view of history and psychology. In its most mechanical forms, *Marxist* criticism concerns itself with those aspects of a work which mirror the "class struggle" or further it, and *Freudian* criticism with those aspects of a work which illustrate its author's agreement (conscious or not) with Freudian doctrine. Freudian criticism has paid some works (such as Sophocles' *Oedipus*) the compliment of seeing in them early perceptions of "permanent truths" about humanity. At their best both kinds of criticism have been valuable, with Marxist criticism helping us understand the social implications of a work, and Freudian criticism helping explain an author's manipulation of psychological themes.

The work of Freud's associate and later his rival in psychological research and theory, Carl Jung, has also had an important influence on recent literary criticism. Jung's work led him to a deep interest in myth and in the identification of archetypal characters and situations. The kind of literary criticism that builds upon Jung's views and examines literature in terms of archetype and myth is often called, appropriately enough, *myth criticism* or *archetypal criticism*. Its value lies in its power to suggest what depths of consciousness are plumbed by the writer when he achieves profound responses. But its weakness lies in its inability to provide a literary basis for distinguishing between good literature and bad, and in its emphasis on writings which are sometimes of doubtful literary value despite their relevance to myth. However, it is possible, as Northrop Frye does in his influential book *The Anatomy of Criticism,* to base a synoptic or summary view of the whole of literature by indicating the various relations of specific works to the myth cycle.

In addition to these varieties of criticism, there are others which, while based primarily on the proposition that literature is an *esthetic object,* go beyond an exclusive concern with its internal structural relations. The criticism of Kenneth Burke and R. P. Blackmur does this. The traditional French *explication de texte,* calling on history, philosophy, and biography to explain the relations of language, idea, and form in a work, has been an influential example for many critics. Some varieties of esthetic criticism concern themselves with the application of ideas of beauty derived from philosophy to the understanding of the internal relations of a work. Others, such as the so-called *New Criticism* or the *ontological criticism* envisioned by John Crowe

Ransom, are generally concentrated on the internal relations of a work.

Finally, there is a variety of criticism in which the critic is his own law, though ultimately he bases his procedure on the proposition that literature is a *cause*. This is *impressionist criticism,* in which the critic examines the effects of a work on himself, observing the behavior of a soul (his own) adventuring among masterpieces—to paraphrase Anatole France.

The most frequent objection to impressionist criticism is that it is only as good as the critic who employs it. But this objection may be made to any sort of critical approach—the sensitivity of the critic is decisive. Literary criticism has produced no triumphs of system over stupidity. On the contrary, great critical essays are often the result of the critic's willingness to sacrifice rigid method and to follow where his insights lead. Yet if the value of actual criticism depends on the sensitivity of the critic, the value we see in the various premises about how literature may be understood depends, in great measure, on what kinds of value we see in literature itself.

PREMISES FOR EVALUATING LITERATURE

The premises on which literature is commonly evaluated are suggested in Horace's often quoted phrase on the goals of poetry: *aut prodesse ... aut delectare,* "either to profit or delight." Literature may be of profit in presenting a *knowledge* or *criticism* of life or in acting as a *cause* of beneficial changes in men or society. It may delight by satisfying *esthetic standards* proper to the several kinds of literature. An individual work is judged to be good or bad according to the extent to which it achieves these ends.

The relations among these premises have been viewed in several recurrent ways. There are those who believe the premises either identical or in some way harmonious. For Platonists, who accept the identity of the True, the Good, and the Beautiful, the relation of the premises is simple, sometimes devastatingly so. For others, such as the neo-Aristotelian critic Elder Olson, there is a harmony rather than an identity in the premises. "The ethical function of art is, therefore, never in opposition to the purely artistic end. . . . The same thing is true of any political or social ends of art, provided that the state be a good state or the society a moral society." However, the brutal contexts of the last half-century seem to turn Mr. Olson's last provision into a complete denial.

Another way of relating the premises has been to see some as requisite to others. Thus, critics primarily interested in ethical matters have looked upon a work's pleasurable effects and its satisfaction of esthetic standards as means to an ethical end: "sugar-coating the pill of truth," as a Puritan critic said. In other critics a different view prevails. Dr. Johnson, for example, looked upon truth as "one of the general conditions of pleasure."

The premises of judgment have also been viewed as in conflict with one another or as of greater or less importance. Some critics have adopted the position that only one premise is of any importance and all the others are irrelevant. Father Gerard Manley Hopkins seemed convinced of a conflict between the ethical and esthetic ends of literature in the following passage from a letter to Canon Dixon:

> Our Society [the Jesuits] values, as you say, and has contributed to literature, to culture; but only as a means to an end. Its history and its experience shew that literature proper, as poetry, has seldom been found to be to that [ethical] end a very serviceable means.

And similarly, in his commentary on Dryden's poem *Absalom and Achitophel*, Dr. Johnson states that if the poem is considered "political and controversial, it will be found to comprise all the excellencies of which the subject is susceptible" but that if the poem is considered from an esthetic standpoint, "there is an unpleasant disproportion between the beginning and the end."

An example of a critic who finds the premises of unequal value is I. A. Richards. In his book *Practical Criticism*, Mr. Richards states that "It is less important to like 'good' poetry and dislike 'bad' than to be able to use them both as a means of ordering our minds." This clearly implies that the value of a work should be judged primarily according to its beneficial effect on the reader, rather than according to its esthetic qualities.

An example of a "monistic" approach to literary judgment is the often quoted passage from Archibald MacLeish's poem, "Ars Poetica":

> A poem should not mean
> But be.[2]

The lines have been widely used as a motto for the view that a poem's value lies in its being an esthetic object rather than a source of knowledge about life or a criticism of it.

Such are the major ways of relating the three most important premises on which literary evaluations are based. We may now proceed to an examination of the soundness of the premises themselves.

LITERATURE AS KNOWLEDGE

The extent and kind of knowledge literature can offer has been a subject of frequent dispute. Works of literature have been praised for their accuracy and vitality as representations of men and events and for their ability to evoke in the reader a view of men and events apart from his own self-interest. On the other hand, the supposed accuracy of literature has been labeled an *illusion of reality* rather than *realism,* and its vitality has been attributed not to the accurate representation of life but rather to the emotional intensity with which the reader is led to contemplate the work. In other words, it has been argued that literature does not give us knowledge, but that it manipulates our feelings so that we accept as knowledge what is only an artistic organization of details whose truth or falsity is irrelevant to their effect. It was partly on this basis—the unreliability of literature's representation of knowledge, especially knowledge of the Good—that Plato thought of eliminating poets from his ideal republic. He is not the last to whom the idea has occurred.

At another extreme, the poet Shelley felt that "A poem is the very image of life expressed in its eternal truth . . . the creation of actions according to the unchangeable forms of human nature, as existing in the mind of the creator, which is itself

2 From *Streets in the Moon* by Archibald MacLeish (Boston: Houghton Mifflin Company, 1926), p. 38.

the image of all other minds." Few people would now accept
the idea that the writer's mind is the image of all other minds,
though more might agree that the forms of human nature do
not change rapidly. However, Shelley's notion of eternal truths
is, in most applications, open to serious objection. Somewhere
the dramatist Ibsen says that a good truth lasts about eighteen
years. In any case, even when Shelley's remarks are thought
of as relating to psychological or ethical "truth," they seem
unduly hopeful.

Familiarity with literary works leads us to a sense of their
limitations as sources of knowledge. Since literature cannot
ordinarily offer proof of either a deductive or empirical sort,
such information as it presents is often only corroborative. Further, successful works of literature rarely present great numbers
of "facts" about a single subject. Aristotle found poetry more
philosophic than history because it expressed univerals rather
than particulars. Some ancient Greek scientific treatises, however, *are* written metrically; works of the eighteenth century
which critics now only reluctantly call poems deal in detail with
sheep-raising or farming, and recent novels frequently plod
through the minutiae of such activities as the manufacture of
ladies' undergarments. But Aristotle called the Greek philosopher Empedocles a physicist despite his meter. And generally
such works as his are now considered either not to be literature
at all or to be so in spite of, rather than because of, their extensive "information."

We do not ordinarily consider literature as a source of
knowledge because in literature the transmission of accurate
information seems subordinate to other ends. In a historical
work the attribution of the "discovery" of the Pacific to Cortez
would be greeted by amusement—first at the obvious European
chauvinism of the attribution, and second because Balboa was
probably the first European to reach the Pacific coast. Yet
Keats' attribution of the "discovery" to "stout Cortez" is more
frequently considered a minor curiosity than a flaw in his sonnet on Chapman's translation of Homer. Again, in an account
of history we would expect an author to limit himself to whatever is actually known about historical figures, even if what is
known is insufficient to convey a sense of individual identity.
We would look with misgivings on a historian who invented

"facts" to round out his pictures of men. However, a failure to attempt this sort of "invention" of personality would be almost surely fatal in fiction or drama. The method of expository writing lies in its proposing no organization of information not logically justified by the information available. But the method of a work of literature lies in its presenting no "information" which does not further a significant esthetic organization. Other writing demands, primarily, respect of fact; literature demands, primarily, respect of imaginative or esthetic order.

Even if we assume that ultimately there is an order for all facts, we are unlikely to discover it. Therefore, conflicting claims are bound to arise between a primary concern for fact and a primary concern for esthetic order; between, in other words, informative writing and literature. We can deal with this distinction by saying (as do Shelley and others) that the order literature presents suggests the ultimate order and, therefore, that art is a form of ultimate knowledge. But the same facts can be disposed in many kinds of esthetically successful order. And many kinds of esthetic order can be created simply by neglect or ignorance of some or many facts. It is no dispraise of literature to say that it is not ultimate knowledge. On the contrary, this is a kind of optimism. If we had to await final knowledge, the pleasures of literature would be denied us forever.

To judge literature solely as knowledge, then, seems like trying a man by the laws of another country. There are certain kinds of knowledge literature cannot convey, or can convey only at its greatest peril—dullness. In addition, its requirement of order may cause the author to leap beyond current knowledge or even beyond what is possible, as in fantasy. However, this is not to deny the importance of literature as a source of certain kinds of knowledge, especially knowledge of human behavior, or the importance of knowledge as a means to other ends in literature.

It is not to deny that literature—unlike the sciences or social studies—gives us whole images of man, and is thus more accurate in conveying a sense of the whole tenor of life. It is not to deny that literature gives us unique insights into human situations that escape ethical or logical categories.[3] It is not even

3　On these points see Chapters I and IV.

to deny that a phrase or a fable has the power to shock us into a recognition of wisdom. It is merely to say that this premise has serious limitations and can lead, at best, to only a partial judgment of literature. At worst, it can lead to the rejection of works whose major failing is that their authors knew no more of the universe than Ptolemy and no more of medicine than Galen.

There is, however, another way of viewing literature as knowledge. A work may be valued for the insight it gives us into the times of its author or into the author himself. It may be valued, therefore, as an effect of social and psychological causes. But this premise for literary judgment also has limitations. Again, the historical or psychological knowledge it imparts may be of little value without other information. An unfortunate circularity that afflicts some historical critics is the characterization of a period on the basis of its literature and, then, the praise of individual works for accurately "reflecting" that period. Generally, the evaluation of a work on the basis of the historical insight it affords neglects the elements of subjectivity and craftsmanship in literature. Literature gives us not merely the world, but the world as seen by a particular personality, and not only this vision, but this vision as manipulated for ends other than that of historical accuracy. There is the French Revolution of Carlyle's essay and of Burke's, of Dickens' *Tale of Two Cities*, of Wordsworth's poems and of Coleridge's—and then there is the French Revolution, a complex circumstance of history whose details and meaning are still in dispute. To judge a work on the basis of historical accuracy is to assume that we possess a nearly final knowledge of some segment of history (which, in itself, is doubtful) and also to assume an overly simple relation between a work of literature and its times. Similar objections may be lodged against the attempt to value a work as a simple document imparting psychological knowledge of its author.

Yet these arguments can cut both ways. Historians may develop only imperfect views of an age if they neglect the transmutation of its qualities and issues into literature. And a close reading of literary works may provide the basis for an "interior" history or biography far more sensitive and complete than accounts based only on "hard" documents. In cautious and sophisticated hands, literature has yielded important knowledge of men and events. An inevitable part of such caution and sophistication, however, is the recognition that literature is more than knowledge and perhaps only a dubious source of it. This, in turn, means a recognition that other ways of evaluating literary works are at least as significant as the evaluation of literature as knowledge.

LITERATURE AS A CRITICISM OF LIFE

The strengths and limitations of the view that literature is to be valued as a criticism of life are different from those of the premise just discussed. The possible conflicts between the primacy of fact and the primacy of esthetic order do not apply here. Criticisms of life, whether expressed through ethical systems or ideal societies, are themselves kinds of order which, at their most sophisticated, approach the completeness and coherence of art.

But conflicts of another sort are apparent when literature is valued as a statement of ethical or social values. Just as Aristotle viewed poetry as less particular than history, so he viewed it as less universal than philosophy. Literature imparts its criticisms of life primarily through particulars—that is, through character and action. Because of this it can have neither the scope nor the precision of ethical or social views as they are usually stated.

There is a defense of works of literature as value systems parallel to the defense of them as knowledge: that is, on the grounds of vividness. But here again the problem is to decide whether this vividness is due to a work's effectiveness as a system of values or to the intensity with which we contemplate it. In any case, if we consider works of literature as "concrete universals," their concreteness seems to reduce their efficiency as means of imparting value systems, just as their universality seems to reduce their efficiency as means of imparting certain kinds of knowledge.

The sort of practical difficulty encountered in applying the premise that the excellence of a work depends on the completeness and depth of its criticism of life is illustrated in several examples from recent criticism. The Italian critic Croce seems to believe that Dante's *Divine Comedy* is a greater work than any of Shakespeare's because it embodies a more comprehensive and better articulated ethical system. In particular, Croce finds Shakespeare's work deficient in ethical discriminations that can be viewed apart from their contexts in the plays. But this is precisely the point. The danger in the ethical evaluation of literature lies in detaching aspects of a work from the context of the whole. At its worst this may lead not to defensible positions such as Croce's view of Shakespeare but to indefensible ones such as the extravagant praise of works whose only "value" lies in their fine sentiments. A variation of this error arises from a misunderstanding or a failure to see the various contexts in which ethical statements can appear in literature. The praise of honor by the villain Iago and of fidelity by the opportunist Polonius are among the most frequently quoted passages in Shakespeare. But Shakespeare was always putting noble sentiments in the mouths of knaves and fools. This in itself is an ethical judgment—possibly even a judgment detachable from its various contexts in the sense Croce wishes. But such a detachment of Polonius' statements from their context is precisely what can lead to a foolish misunderstanding of this character as a noble sage. He is merely a rather prosy old gentleman.

There is, finally, the possibility that in some works of literature questions of value either will not arise or will be so simple as to be unimportant. Although Milton's aim in *Paradise Lost* was to "justify the ways of God to men," he felt that excellences in poetry derived also from its being "direct, sensuous and passionate." Many poems which, as criticism of life, are shallow or undefined are valuable on precisely the grounds Milton provides. The painter Cezanne said of Manet that he was only an eye—but what an eye! It is possible to say the same of many poets who were capable of no more complex valuative judgments than are implied in an attachment to language and to sensuous delight.

As a way of evaluating literature, then, the view that it is to be judged as a criticism of life has definite limitations. There is not an exact or even close correspondence between the works that have been most highly praised as literature and the works of literature that embody the most profound or complete systems of values. The cult of youth and art in the great odes of Keats is shallow compared to the wisdom of some of the poetry of Santayana, but there is no question as to the relative merits of Keats and Santayana as poets. Nor is there any question that the works of Shakespeare and Dante, to name only two of the greatest writers, are justly valued as criticisms of life. In short, to judge a work of literature as a criticism of life is, at best, to make an important but only a partial judgment of it.

LITERATURE AS A CAUSE OF CHANGE

We may see a close relation between judging a work as a criticism of life and judging it as a cause of beneficial changes in men and society if we presume that an embodiment of ethical and social ideals in a work will move men to change themselves and their surroundings. Thus the pathos and satire of Dickens' *Nicholas Nickleby* are viewed as causes of the reforms of Yorkshire boarding schools, and the dubious humanitarianism of *Uncle Tom's Cabin* is viewed as a cause of the Civil War. Both views are exaggerated. It is unlikely that a literary work has actually been the *cause* of any significant social change, although it may have solidified or intensified already existing opinion on social questions.

Yet one sort of criticism judges works of literature as "weapons" in a social struggle. Hence a novel is thought good if it discourages divorce or promotes the interests of the middle and lower peasantry. It is obvious that those holding such a view would at times employ literature for petty ends or worse. This is not to say that only inferior works have been written for momentary political or personal advantage. Dryden's *Absalom and Achitophel*, to use only one example, is a poem great in spite of the author's purpose—to break the power of an anti-royalist politician.

But the real objection to the narrowly utilitarian judgment of literature is its confusion of literature with persuasion. Men are moved to action for many reasons, among them narrow self-interest. But it is the nature and excellence of literature to permit us to conceive of experience in the interest of others or at least apart from our own interest. (This formulation may, by the way, be made the basis of a sounder view of how literature is useful.) In any case, persuasion and art rarely lead to similar organizations of detail, and to judge works on the basis of their causing or having the power to cause social change would be to eliminate almost all literature from consideration. The branding of whole bodies of art as "decadent" by totalitarian critics is an illustration of this point.

On the other hand, the view that literature is to be judged according to the changes it effects in individuals is rather more reasonable. But the same work may cause different emotions or degrees of emotion in different men, and the critic employing this premise may mistake the capacities of particular men for the excellence of literature. On the other hand, it is not incorrect to say that literature is one of the means by which man has made himself more human—that it is one of the humanities. Individual works, therefore, may be viewed as promoting various sorts of human sensitivity. But whether this general observation can be made the basis of useful distinctions of excellence among individual works is doubtful. Auden's poem, "On the Death of William Butler Yeats," urges the poet to "Teach the free man how to praise." But whether his poem does this more effectively than, say, Yeats' own poem "Sailing to Byzantium" is a question that leads, of necessity, to so many matters outside literature that it raises the danger of the neglect of the poems themselves.

LITERATURE AS A SOURCE OF PLEASURE

An effective version of the view that literature is to be judged according to how it satisfies natural appetites must depend on a clear formulation of these appetites and the means by which they are appeased. Sometimes the appetites are related to instincts. An example of this is the postulation of a *mimetic instinct* in man which is satisfied by drama or by an "imitation" of reality. This train of speculation may lead from the idea of "imitation" to the judging of works as knowledge of men and events. But more often the concern with the appetites which art satisfies leads critics to construct a standard for artistic form on which individual works are to be judged. Typical of this procedure is some of the criticism of Burke, who moves from the psychology of the audience to the analysis of literary form, and some of the criticism of the neo-Aristotelians, a representative of whom, Elder Olson, states that "pleasure is commensurate

. . . with the beauty of poetic form," and then goes on to define beauty in terms of formal relations in the types of literature.

There are two major strategies by which formal standards of judgment may be arrived at. A critic may set up standards with the widest possible applicability, or he may set up standards that apply only to certain kinds of works or certain phases of works. A work, therefore, may be judged on some general standard, such as the degree to which its form is "organic"— that is, the degree to which its parts demand and satisfy one another. Or it may be judged on standards appropriate to its type. So Arthur Miller's tragedy *Death of a Salesman* may be judged on the basis of Aristotle's formal criteria for tragedy.

The possible deficiencies of such procedures are obvious. A general standard may be too general to be meaningful. This is one of the difficulties with such frequently invoked standards as *coherence* and *unity*. And a narrow standard may be so narrow as to permit of discriminations among only a few works or a few aspects of works. Hence, we are likely to remain unsatisfied by critical essays, however perceptive, which confine themselves to evaluation of, say, the metaphors in a lyric poem—although such a concern may, and indeed should, lead to a discussion of the context of the metaphors—that is, the whole poem.

In addition, the criticism of works of literature by strictly esthetic standards is sometimes open to the charge of circularity: the standards being deduced from works which are then in turn judged by these standards. However, the varieties of esthetic criticism have the virtue of keeping the work itself, rather than some other subject, almost continually under discussion.

In varying degrees all the premises of literary judgment we have considered can lead to significant evaluations of individual works. On the other hand, all can lead, and have led, some critics nowhere. The capacity to understand the premises of criticism is not the ability to apply them. Some estheticians are peculiarly gifted with bad taste, and some critics who have a great ability to discriminate among works are naïve in abstract discussions of the grounds of literary judgment. About all we can ask of particular esthetic theories is that they obscure as few great works of art as possible and that, by defining its varieties, they help us undergo the active experience of literature itself.

4 5 6 7 8 9 10 11 12 13 14 15 16 17 18 19 20 21 22 23 24 25   SH   74 73 72 71 70 69